KNOWING

ISBN: 978-0-9998597-1-1 (Hardcover)
ISBN: 978-0-9998597-0-4 (Paperback)
ISBN: 978-0-9998597-2-8 (Digital Book)

Envoy Publishing
12155 W. Peak View Rd.
Peoria, Arizona 85383

LIBRARY OF CONGRESS CATALOGING-IN-PUBLICATION DATA

Jeffery C. Olsen
Knowing / Jeffery C. Olsen

Library of Congress: Pending

Cover design: Jeffery C. Olsen
Editor: Hannah Lyon - hramarosa@gmail.com
Interior and ePub Design: Dayna Linton, Day Agency

KNOWING

ENVOY

PUBLISHING

www.EnvoyPublishing.com

"He who knows others is wise; he who knows himself is enlightened."

Lao Tzu

ACKNOWLEDGMENTS

To MY SONS: THANK YOU for inspiring me to be a better man.

To TONYA: THANK YOU for teaching me unconditional love.

To MY BROTHERS: THANK YOU for showing up for me in the perfect way, every time.

To MY LITTLE SISTERS: THANK YOU for your depth of character.

To MOM: THANK YOU for listening.

To DAD: THANK YOU for making me strong.

To MY ANGELS: THANK YOU for profound insights, answers, and for your love.

To MY HEART: THANK YOU for healing.

FOREWORD

SINCE 1965, I HAVE interviewed thousands of people from all over the world who have had profound near-death experiences. Jeffery Olsen's story is one of the most amazing I have ever heard. It is scarcely conceivable to me, a medical doctor, that he survived given the overwhelming extent of his injuries. Yet he did survive, overcoming the odds to live a happy, creative life.

As a psychiatrist, I often wonder how some individuals are able to get through devastating physical and emotional injuries that would destroy most of us. Jeffery's life is a dramatic case in point. I am grateful that he produced this fascinating book that will inspire everyone who reads it.

Jeffery's book contains the basic elements of high drama: a terrifying accident that comes as a bolt out of the blue, the wrenching grief for lost loved ones, and nightmarish pain from horrific injuries and loss of limb. However, his tale is also a glorious journey to the luminous worlds of love beyond death, as well as hope, renewal, and the courage to love again.

I met Jeffery in 2010, and his ordeal has been on my mind ever since. How, I wondered, could anyone manage to live through the catastrophe that befell him? Of course, his profound near-death experience was a factor in his survival, but that is not the whole story. Having met Jeffery, I sense a gentle, thoughtful, determined man whose joy in life is to serve others. I think these qualities come across beautifully in his book.

Jeffery's near-death experience is one of several in recent years that are expanding the frontiers of our understanding of death. The details of what happened to him are so extraordinary that his experiences are a real challenge to explain in mundane terms. Jeffery is a pioneer in a way, venturing out to the borderlands where life meets death, bringing back news of a life hereafter. I suspect that Jeffery and a few others like him are moving us closer than we have ever before been to the Holy Grail of rational inquiry—real evidence of life after death.

Raymond Moody, PhD, MD
www.lifeafterlife.com

Dedicated to my angels, seen and unseen

PREFACE

I'VE SAT DOWN AND stared at my computer screen countless times only to decide that I have said enough. I've told my story and therefore have nothing more to share. That feels comfortable to me, if comfort is what one looks for in life. I'd quite like to be finished. Truthfully, I don't enjoy writing at all; I find it exhausting. Choosing words to communicate the things I've experienced and what I've learned can be soul-stretching. The vulnerability is uncomfortable as well. Writing and sharing such personal things feels like dancing naked across a stage in front of strangers, or, worse yet, in front of people I know.

However, at the core of my soul, I know there is more to say about what I've learned. So, I've chosen to let go of the irrelevant judgment of others. What matters is how I feel, and I know there is more to share.

If a drunk driver ran us off the road, killing my wife and youngest child, I could forgive that person. If our vehicle was tossed across the freeway by powerful crosswinds, I could forgive God. But if I fell asleep at the wheel, then I am accountable and therefore must respond in an accountable way.

We were northbound on I-15 at about one o'clock in the afternoon, returning from a family vacation in southern Utah. The cruise control was set at seventy-five miles per hour when the vehicle veered sharply to the right, crossing over the speed ratchets and onto the gravel along the side of the road. I overcorrected, causing the car to flip back up onto the hard asphalt. Then it rolled seven or eight complete revolutions.

When our car finally tumbled to a stop, my wife, Tamara, age thirty-one, and my fourteen-month-old son, Griffin, were dead. My seven-year-old son, Spencer, was in the backseat, crying for help but at least alive. As for myself, I was crammed under the steering column. Both of my legs were crushed my ribs broken. I gasped for air and bled from the gash the seat belt had cut through my lower abdomen and hip.

Though I was conscious, I could barely see through all the blood in my eyes. I attempted to wipe it out, but I couldn't get my arms to work either. Perhaps it would have been easier for me if I'd had someone else to blame. There were reports of a red truck driving recklessly in the same area that day, but I don't remember a red truck. There were weather reports of wind gusts over a hundred miles per hour, but I don't remember the wind. I don't necessarily remember falling asleep at the wheel either, but the fact remains that I was driving the car. I had no one to blame but myself.

It all happened at mile marker 80, which may not seem like a sacred or noteworthy place. It's only a signpost on a lonely stretch of highway about two and a half hours north of Las Vegas. For me, however, it's both the beginning and ending point of a painful and glorious journey; painful because of what I experienced, and glorious because of what I learned. Pain can often be the carrier pigeon of wisdom, and wisdom brings peace. But make no mistake that both come with a price and are found only at the end of a path every soul chooses to travel.

I once read a story about a potter who would create beautiful pots. He would glaze them with fantastic finishes, only to wrap them in burlap and break them into hundreds of pieces. Then he would meticulously reassemble the pieces back together, filling the cracks with contrasting colors and even precious metals. When asked why he did such a thing, he explained that the process was what made each pot unique. It made them interesting and gave them character.

How does one reassemble a life? Mine had been crushed into so many pieces I felt I could never find them all, let alone put them back together. I was sure I was losing my mind as I attempted to find "normal" again. Raising my surviving son, Spencer, alone was a challenge. Being productive at work and masking my grief was a battle. Dealing with my physical injuries and rehabilitation was an ongoing uphill climb.

Perhaps I didn't realize how much support I was receiving all along the way. I waded through the mayhem, barely holding on, but in hindsight, I see how many angels came to assist me. Some were family, friends, and neighbors. Others were very much from a heavenly realm, but they came to heal, guide, comfort, and direct me. I learned how to listen, trust, and find peace. Eventually, I recognized the miracles that had been so evident in my life—the biggest being that I finally decided to choose joy even in difficult circumstances, and that made all the difference.

Perhaps our lives are like those pots. Only when we are shattered and reassembled, do we step into our true glory as one of God's unique masterpieces.

CHAPTER 1

I REMEMBER LIGHT. IT STREAMED in between the seams of the curtains in our front room picture window, creating dancing patterns on the hardwood floors of our little rambler house. I was hunched behind the couch because the world didn't make sense to me anymore. Mom and Dad were splitting up, and my four-year-old heart couldn't comprehend why.

It was 1969, and Marvin Gaye was singing, "I Heard It Through The Grapevine." I didn't know what that meant, but the rumor around our house was that my brothers and I would be leaving with Mom to live in Salt Lake City. I was too young to fully understand, but I knew it hurt and filled me with anxiety and insecurity.

I remember how dark the night felt. It was the kind of darkness that reaches beyond the eyes and into the soul, causing my spirit to feel dim. Almost in the same way light extends from its source, this darkness seemed to expand from my heart and into the overcast night-time sky. No moon, no stars. There was only emptiness and anxiety as we packed the car with the few things we could carry, loaded up the family dog, and backed out of the driveway of what had been home. My mom bedded us down in the backseat, but I lay awake watching the streetlights move across the car window as we passed underneath them.

My older brother, Jed, was angry about what was happening. He was only seven, but he understood more than I did. I always looked up to him and felt safe when he was around. He had dark brown eyes and nearly jet-black hair, which was kept very short in a butch style haircut. He reminded me of my favorite G.I. Joe action figure, which I held tightly in my hand as I felt the car accelerate onto the interstate.

Inside the car was silent. My mom didn't speak, the radio was not on, and Jed was very still in the front passenger seat with his arms folded and his head laid against the car door. The only sound was the tires on the wet road and the occasional swoosh of traffic moving around outside. I watched the street lights from my vantage point in the back seat, looking up at them from the back window as I did my best to lay quiet and fake that I was asleep, too.

My three-year-old brother, Justin, lay next to me. We were best pals. He still had his baby fat, and I stroked his chubby cheek and played with his earlobe as he slept. I felt responsible for him somehow. I know it was my own anxiety I was feeling, but I wanted to protect him from all the insecurity I was experiencing.

My parents' divorce became final four months later. My brothers and I grew up fast over those next few years. My mom had to take a job, so the three of us looked after each other until she got home each night. We still saw plenty of my dad. He had remarried, but he remained dedicated to his children. We spent every weekend with him on the farm.

My parents were amicable over the divorce and shared custody. My mom didn't mind my dad spending time with us. They both spoke highly of each other and were kind toward one another in our presence; in fact, our parents didn't even fight.

I never heard judgment from my mom over the decisions my dad had made, and my father spoke of my mother with reverence. However, my dad's second marriage didn't last, which added greatly to my insecurities and trust issues. My father felt a lot of remorse over what had transpired in two failed marriages, but remained dedicated to the wellbeing of his children.

My mom eventually remarried when my brothers and I were all in our teens. She had dated on and off over the seven years while she was single, but my brothers and I made sure we chased all mom's courters my brothers

and I made sure we chased all mom's courters away. I'm not sure if it was jealousy or fear, which often feel so much alike, but we teased my mother—sometimes in cruel ways—after every date she ever went on. We'd laugh and poke fun, but then proceeded to tell her in very sober tones how awful the guys were that she was seeing, no matter who they were or how they acted.

We did not make it easy for her. I suppose we liked having things the way they were, with our mom all to ourselves. To me, it felt like I had lost too much already, and if Mom were to fall in love with another man, that would in some way take away the only thing that felt secure in my life: her love and devotion to me and my brothers.

After several years, she finally met a man who was worth making a fresh start with, and by then my brothers and I had matured enough to see that he made her happy, so we acquiesced to their relationship and eventual marriage.

Jed was starting high school at the time, and he moved out to live with my dad on the farm as soon as my mom got remarried. He had been assuming the man of the house role over those many years, and I think it was uncomfortable for him when our mother tied the knot again.

Jed encouraged Justin and me to move in with him and our dad permanently. Jed felt we boys were meant to stick together, to be a family. The three of us had become just that over the years with mom working and only visiting my dad on weekends. Even though we had good parents, my brothers and I had spent a lot of time alone together. Jed had become the authority figure for both Justin and I; what he said ruled. He had already primed us for staying on the farm after the summer break. My mom was expecting us to return to the city to start school that fall, but we made a different plan.

It was out in the hay barn where the definitive conversation took place. Somehow, talks between brothers always seemed to go down there behind those hallowed slat boards and beneath those lofty rafters. There was an honesty about that old barn that somehow held the context for getting down to the truth of any matter.

Jed laid it out plain and simple that night after all the chores were done. Dad needed our help with the farm work and we were big enough now to make a difference. Paying people to do the work we could do was silly. Besides, we'd do a much better job because it was our home. He was making a logical argument, but the bottomline was that we were family and brothers didn't split up. Jed had already spent one full year on his own with my dad and it was the earnestness in his eyes that seemed to say, "I want you here with me."

That's what made all the difference.

That very night, Justin and I decided to follow in Jed's footsteps and stay on the farm. My single dad welcomed the notion of having us with him full-time. I was thirteen, and Justin was twelve, but we were growing into strong young men. I was actually torn by this decision at the time. I liked the city and had big plans to play on the local Skyline High School football team, which had been a state powerhouse for years. I was going into the eighth grade and only a few years away from realizing that dream.

My brothers and I had all been involved in Little League football and baseball and had become good athletes. Mom was our biggest cheerleader. Sports kept us occupied and out of trouble while she worked to support us as a single mother. I know it hurt my mom when we packed up and moved ourselves onto the farm with our dad, but we were committed to continuing the bond that had welded us as brothers over those volatile years.

In addition to farming, my father was in the military, and he would go on active duty from time to time, leaving us three teenage boys to do the farm work and to run the entire operation. It taught us responsibility yet put a lot of pressure on us, especially Jed. We'd fight sometimes, and even ended up throwing punches, but through it all my brothers were my best friends. They always had my back, and I had theirs.

We worked hard on the farm. We had over a hundred cows to milk three times every day, along with their calves to raise and take care of. Putting up enough feed for them was quite a chore too. We also had horses, a few pigs, and a small herd of beef cattle to care for as well. Days began at 4:00 A.M.. and consisted of pulling on boots and overalls on our way out the back door with our eyes still half closed to brave the cold early morning air.

The pungent smell of dairy always brought consciousness swiftly, and by the time I'd reach the barn I was usually wide awake and ready to go. Herding the cows who weren't already waiting for milking up to the barn was always interesting. Steam would roll off of their large bodies as they rose to their feet from their straw beds.

In the deep cold of winter, I would often lay against them as they walked to allow the heat from their big bodies to warm mine. Summer was different; we spent nearly all day shirtless, wearing nothing but boots and jeans while we worked the fields and put up crops in every spare hour between milking and feeding the cows.

We'd sometimes take short breaks to grab an easy, hand-held lunch and fish the upper Provo River, which bordered our property. We kept a couple of small poles behind the seat of the farm truck and could easily make our way up and down the river for a few minutes while on the lower end of our acreage.

My brother and I had great luck and caught all we could eat for dinner without my dad even noticing we'd been away. There was a wildness on the farm that was perfect for growing boys. However, I used to be jealous of the other kids from school when they would go down to Deer Creek Reservoir to water ski and play on the water while I was hauling hay or milking cows. In the end, all that hard work with animals, machinery, and my boisterous brothers formed not only my developing muscles but also my values. What I once wished away now has become what I wish for; that every boy could have a farm to raise him.

I learned a lot about life during those years. I remember watching a farmhand named Ben work with horses in our corral. Ben showed up one day looking for work. He was a handsome but rugged man, soft-spoken, probably in his mid-thirties. He was a Native American, but I don't remember him mentioning which tribe he belonged to. He told my dad he had no money and would work for food and a place to sleep.

My father had a kind heart and had nothing against hiring folks who deserved a break. Dad asked him what kind of work he did, and Ben said he liked working with horses. We happened to have three two-year-old colts that needed breaking, so my dad told Ben he could start with them. He didn't tell Ben how to break horses. I suppose we were all interested in seeing how he might go about it on his own.

Ben looked at the horses for a while, then climbed into the small corral where the colts were. The young horses whinnied and scrambled near the back fence, putting as much distance as possible between themselves and Ben as he made his way through the gate and into the center of the corral.

I was up in the barn hayloft, watching Ben through the wood slats. I took off my sweaty leather gloves and nestled in next to a soft bale of straw at the far corner of the loft that had broken open during the past winter. I could comfortably rest and watch what happened from there without making any noise or being noticed. I turned my ball cap backwards so I could lay my face right up against the wood slats to see better through the small opening. There was Ben, standing very still dead center of the corral.

He did nothing while the horses wandered around the perimeter of the fenceline, looking for a way out. Occasionally, they'd look back at Ben. He stood there quietly and stretched out his arms like a human scarecrow. He started to talk to the colts, softly and calmly. I couldn't understand what he was saying, but he moved his arms in slow, circular motions as he chanted and sang to the horses. Finally, one colt moved closer to him, seemingly becoming curious about what Ben was doing.

Ben continued to speak softly to the horse, not in English but in his native tongue. I didn't comprehend a word he said, but the tone of his voice was kind and soothing, like a song. I watched for what seemed like hours, amazed at what I was witnessing. It was as if he was dancing with the young horse. He didn't have a bucket of grain, a rope, or anything else at this point; Ben just simply opened arms and moved them gracefully. I leaned back to get in a more comfortable position and waved away the dust I had stirred up from the old straw bale to keep a clear view.

This was not the way I had seen horses broken to ride before. Typically, Dad tied them up and let them learn how to respect a lead rope and halter. He taught them who was boss, so to speak. Ben's method was markedly different; he actually talked them into what he wanted. As I watched, I was learning something profound: language was more than words; it was also energy and intent. It wasn't what Ben was saying or how he was moving, but the energy behind it, around it, and about it that made all the difference.

After a while, Ben actually lay down on his back right down in the dirt, looking up at the sky. He remained in that position for a while, his patience seemingly endless. Gradually, the horses all moved closer, perhaps because he appeared less threatening stretched out on the ground like that. He looked stoic, almost dead, just lying there in the dirt and chaff of the corral. The tone of his skin matched the brownish soil. I noticed the soles of his worn cowboy boots and how one of them actually had what looked like a hole in the bottom.

I wondered if that was perhaps all he had; the boots, jeans, pearl-button western shirt, and cowboy hat he had hung on a fence post by the gate. He never appeared desperate, although perhaps poor. He was confident in what he was doing even though to me it made no conventional sense at all.

Finally, the horses came close enough to sniff Ben's face and chest. Slowly, Ben raised his hand and stroked the sides of their faces, then their soft noses, and other parts of their heads. It wasn't long until he was stroking their forelegs too.

Slowly, Ben got to his feet. When the horses started to worry and move away, Ben would wait quietly until they returned. After rubbing their necks and backs for a long time, he leaned against one of their shoulders and slowly pushed his chest and stomach onto the horse's back.

He was coaxing the horses to trust him. Ben allowed them to take their time and become comfortable with him in a way that bonded them as equal partners, rather than as dominant master over beast.

I eventually worked my way stealthily out of the barn and back to the work I knew my father expected to be done before the end of the day. I thought about what I had seen while I fed the small calves and watered the other farm animals. Ben worked with the horses into the night, long after we went in for the evening. In the morning, he was right back at it at first light. Most likely, he'd slept in the corral and spent the night with them. By the end of the third day, Ben was actually riding all three horses. He used a hackamore-style headstall that didn't cause any pain when he applied rein pressure to the horse's head. They ended up being some of the best horses we ever had.

I learned a lot watching Ben. In addition to teaching me about patience, he demonstrated a heart-to-heart language not found in dictionaries. He spoke in terms of spirit or energy, which was universal. I witnessed how the horses responded to it, and realized it was almost the same when Ben walked onto the farm and asked my dad for work. He had an energy about him that communicated volumes without words.

That may have been the first time I remember feeling something beyond this world. It was something powerful, yet still and calm. The way Ben had communicated with the animals, not with words but with energy and intention, was something I never forgot.

CHAPTER 2

MY BROTHERS AND I continued playing sports in between our farm chores. All that physicality taught me to appreciate my body. I was strong and fast and could work long hours without getting tired. Even when the work was done, our recreation usually involved sports of some kind.

One of my favorite things to do in the summer was to run as fast as I could down our dirt lane to the river. I'd pump my arms and legs forward as far as I could, feeling the ground roll under my feet as I pushed into each stride. I loved sucking in the cool, country air laced with the scent of trees and the river. I especially loved the smell of the air when we were putting up alfalfa. I would run out into the hayfields at night, stretch myself out on a bale of hay, and look up into the star-filled sky.

I wondered about life, unbothered by the sharpness of the cold night air as I lay there for hours. I thought about God and the deeper questions that float around in the head of a teenage boy. What was God like? Did he have a wife or was he single like my dad? I felt God must care about me at some level, if there was a God. I had been taught that God was real and something about those wide-open fields and the infinite number of stars in the sky told me it was so.

I didn't go to church much as a boy, though my mom was a devout member of the Mormon church. Since we spent most weekends with my dad, who had temporarily left the faith, I didn't spend a lot of Sundays in the church pews. My mom read scriptures to us and taught us how to pray. My dad instilled honor and integrity, even if it was with a good kick in the pants from time to time. But my religious views and spiritual opinions came mostly from what I felt in my heart or from what I saw in nature.

From a very young age I had been observant of how things worked in nature. I noticed the instincts of animals, even little birds and how they always seemed to know what to do and where to go. Even before I began kindergarten, I realized that if I was very still, my heart seemed to know what to do as well, just like the instincts in those animals I often watched.

Trusting outside of myself had become an issue, though. Aside from my brothers, I often didn't know who or what I could count on. The divorces I'd watched my dad go through affected me. Seeing what I believed to be forever vanish, caused doubt and insecurity in how I interacted with other people. I often had to take a deep breath, letting go of that fear, and concentrate on feeling my instincts.

If I had any religion as a boy, I suppose it was athletics. My first love was baseball and I played right up until moving back on the farm with my dad. In high school, I wrestled, rode bareback bronc horses on the rodeo team and loved playing football. But by my senior year, I became a one-sport athlete, and all my devotion transferred to football only. It worked out well, because it ended up being my ticket into college, where I received a scholarship to play for Utah State University. I had no aspiration of becoming a professional football player. I was too small and perhaps not fast enough, but I was thankful to play at a Division 1 level at a good university and have my school expenses covered.

My true desire was to become a professional artist. I had always loved to sketch and paint, and my mom told me I drew before I spoke. She even kept a few of the silly little drawings I had done in kindergarten. Back then, my subject matter was typically our family, and my drawings would always include both Mom and Dad, even after they didn't live together anymore. Somewhere in my heart, I held onto the ideal of what family meant and what it might be like to live in a home that still had both a mom and a dad in it. I had spent so much of my life with a single parent that my feelings about what a marriage must be like were completely fantasized.

I started my college courses as a fine art major, but it was difficult to meet the requirements of the program while maintaining an athletic scholarship. Team activities often began as early as 6:00 A.M., before classes started. With practice, team dinner, game films, and study hall, it was often 10:00 P.M. before my team obligations were complete. It wasn't until then that I could start painting to keep up with my art assignments. Sometimes I'd be up all night just to meet basic course requirements, much less to go the extra mile.

Eventually, as part of my core creative study, I took an advertising design class. There I could sketch, draw, and come up with quick, exciting visuals. It was less time-consuming than the fine art courses I had been involved with, but it still fed my creative hunger. I fell in love with my new-found outlet for concepts beyond what could take shape on a traditional canvas. I loved creating clever campaigns, then doing quick sketches and layouts to bring them to life. I found I could squeeze it all in timewise with my athletic demands and still excel at it.

Success was important to me. I was driven to exceed expectations. My father may have played a role in that. I was competitive as well, based on my athletic sensibilities and being raised in a home of all males, but I also had an internal, almost maniacal motivator. The truth was that deep down inside I felt insecure.

Perhaps it was the divorce that made me feel like this, but from the time I was in grammar school I had a nagging belief that I simply was not good enough. I hid it well for the most part, beyond being shy and somewhat introverted. But I wanted to prove to the world and to myself that I was worthwhile. There was a deep desire for self-validation, to prove wrong my nagging thoughts of inadequacy. Yet, no matter how much I tried, I still felt like I came up short. Perhaps I simply never accepted myself.

My insecurities convinced me that I had to work harder and outdo everyone in order to make myself worthwhile. I was popular enough and had lots of good friends, but because of my inferiority complex, I spent a lot of time alone.

I didn't date often. In addition to being shy, I didn't have much money to take girls out. It wasn't that I wasn't interested in girls; I was, far too much at times. But there was that self-judging voice in my head that kept me from getting overly involved, telling me that I was stupid, that I smelled like the farm, or that I would embarrass myself in some way.

It wasn't until I met Tamara Spencer that I began to finally let all those insecurities go. She accepted me the way I was, and that inspired me to begin to accept myself.

CHAPTER 3

I RECALL THE FIRST TIME I saw Tamara, I was a junior in college. The fall semester was just getting underway and all the new students were moving in. Classes would not begin until the following Monday, but I had already been on campus for weeks for summer football drills.

Near the stadium was a student apartment complex, so I walked over with a couple of teammates to see if we might recognize anyone. The evening air was cool, and a delightful break from the late August sun, which had already begun to set, creating a golden sky that backlit everything in view. One of my buddies kicked an empty soda can, clanking it down the street as we crossed the main road from the football stadium to the apartment complex.

When we arrived, we found the names of all the new students posted on a roster near the mailboxes, which made it easy to see who was moving in for fall semester. I scanned the page and, sure enough, saw the name of a girl I had known from high school. My football buddies had all been recruited from California and didn't know any women on campus at all, so they really wanted me to introduce them to some local girls.

Peer pressure finally convinced me to go to the apartment. I hesitated again at the front door, not wanting to knock. The heckling from the other guys became far worse than the outcome of knocking on the door could ever be, so I mustered up the nerve to tap three times on the wooden apartment door. We were pleasantly greeted by a girl I didn't know. She informed us that the girl I was looking for had not arrived yet. It didn't much matter; my more aggressive friends had already stepped into that apartment unit and started small talk, not only with the girl at the door, but with any girls in the unit or even passing by.

Being the shy one, I stepped into the unit and took a seat on the couch in the front room to simply watch the whole ritual. My attention was diverted from my buddies and their antics to a girl coming down the first flight of stairs, carrying a stack of books with a laundry basket balanced on top. She bent down to set her load on the landing. I was mesmerized as she continued down the stairs and walked into the living room.

I actually felt her energy as she entered. She captivated me. She had stunning, sky-blue eyes and natural blonde, shoulder-length hair. The details of her face were soft but striking and well defined. She was thin but shapely and had moved down the stairs with the grace of an angel. Her long legs made her appear tall as she approached.

There was strength and confidence about this girl. She carried a presence that both uncontrollably drew me in and intimidated me. Then she looked over at me. Her glance shot an invigorating jolt through my entire being. I wanted to speak to her but didn't know what to say. "Hello" would have been the obvious, but I could only sit in silence, watching her.

I felt a sudden burst of adrenaline. A little bit of sweat broke out at the small of my back, and that quickly turned into fear and panic. Yet all those emotions were wrapped up in a blanket of calm at the same time. Every feeling I ever knew came rushing through my spine and rippled out into the tips of my toes and fingers.

I nervously stroked backed my hair from my eyes. When I looked at her again, I noticed the corners of her mouth had turned up a bit into a smile as she continued to approach me. It was all in slow motion. The chaos of the other girls and my buddies all around me seemed to vanish like vapor off a lake as the sun comes up in the morning. I was absolutely lost in that moment.

A profound feeling came over me, one that was much deeper than my initial physical attraction: This woman felt familiar in an almost ancient way.

Then my heart jumped within me and said, "This is the woman you are going to marry." I didn't even know her name. Was I crazy? Maybe. But my soul knew her soul in a way that was sudden and indescribable.

"Hey," was all that would come out of my mouth as I stood up from the couch to greet her.

"Hey what?" she asked, as her grin turned into almost a laugh.

"Do you need some help with those books?" *I'm such an idiot*, I thought. *Why can't I say something charming or intelligent?* "I'm Jeff. My friends wanted to come by. We were looking for an old friend of mine, Patty."

"Oh, she won't be here until tomorrow, or so I'm told. I'm new here and don't really know any of these girls. I'm just getting moved in."

I could guess what she was thinking: *these dumb jocks are all alike.* But I wasn't like that. "Well, maybe I can assist you with all that stuff you left on the stairs."

"Maybe, but I'm not sure what to do with it yet."

"What's your name?" I couldn't stop looking at her eyes. They were piercing and so beautiful. I liked the way her mouth moved as she talked. Everything she said had a little smirk to it, as if she were really happy or about to giggle. I watched how her hand moved up to brush back her bangs. "I'm Tamara, but you can call me Tami if you want."

The ice was broken, and I began to relax. She moved over to where she had set her things down and sat on the first step. I sat next to her. I noticed her classic, white tennis shoes and how she wore no socks with them, as well as the delicate nature of her ankles and the way she crossed her feet. I observed the smallness of her hands and the way she often lifted them to her mouth as she spoke, then slightly twisted her hair without ever breaking the trance of the conversation.

My friends had all seemed to disappear, and everyone else in the area quietly left the space (at least on the stairs) to only us. We talked about why she had selected Utah State. She was interested in both business and teaching high school. She knew USU had good programs for both. She had been a state Sterling Scholar winner, meaning she had a full scholarship to any college in the state she wanted to attend. She had almost accepted a slot at Brigham Young University but at the last minute decided to go to Utah State. She said she had a strong feeling it was where she was meant to be.

"So, you don't know anybody here?"

"Nope. Just me. All my friends went to BYU. But I'm sure I'll make good friends here, too."

Her confidence was contagious. She demonstrated the strength I always felt I lacked. We talked into the night, with the conversation flowing easily. Not only was I comfortable around her, which was unusual for me, but I was comfortable with myself when I was with her.

My financial situation caused me to be creative about dating Tamara, which often included the dollar movies, an ice cream bar from the local gas station, and simple walks around campus. It didn't seem to matter, though. It wasn't what we did that was important, but the time we spent together. Our conversations were far more valuable to us than fancy dinners or nights out clubbing. We simply enjoyed each other's company, and that was all we looked forward to.

I didn't kiss her for over a week, and the first time I did it, took us both by surprise. It was not a special date or anything I planned. It happened spontaneously in the parking lot in front of my dormitory. It was getting late; I had walked to her place after football practice. She asked if I wouldn't mind quizzing her for a test she had the next morning. We went through that process very quickly.

She already knew all the answers because she was brilliant, so that turned into a much more enjoyable conversation. She offered to make me dinner, which she did; spaghetti, and it tasted pretty dang good to a starving student athlete. After dinner, she offered to drive me to the football dormitory so I wouldn't have to walk up the campus hill on already tired legs. I welcomed the offer, simply to spend any additional minute I could with her. We walked out into the cool autumn air and hopped into her car.

She started the car, shivered a little bit, looked at me, and said, "Whew, fall is in the air for sure. The heater may not even warm up in the short drive to your place, but I will kick it on anyway."

I watched as she worked the manual transmission of her silver Mustang II. It was fun to just see how she moved. I was totally giddy, a gonner and I knew it. I was so attracted to this girl, both emotionally and physically, that I could barely think straight. Even the ten-minute drive to my dorm was time well spent as I couldn't take my eyes or my mind off of her.

There was no place to park in the dormitory parking lot when we got there, so we simply sat in the car with the engine running to say our good-byes. It was there that she thanked me for helping her study and I thanked her for dinner. It was almost automatic. After I thanked her, I simply leaned over and planted one, softly at first, but then just a little more firm right on her mouth. Everything about it was awkwardly, spontaneously perfect. Despite sitting in the freezing car, it could not have been hotter.

I certainly could have picked a far more romantic spot and time, but the kiss was electrifying all the same. It wasn't long or deep, but it was the catalyst that connected us soul-to-soul in a way that sent sensational energy throughout our physical relationship, not only for the time we dated but also during ten years of marriage. I never got bored.

Tamara was also a devout Mormon. She reminded me of my mother that way. She had a conviction about God and about her connection to the Divine. She brought back so many memories of my childhood and of how my mother had demonstrated her faith through our tough times. Tamara reintroduced me to my own childhood connection to God and to those thoughts I'd had while contemplating the stars in the hayfields at home. She even acquainted me with the church pews again. I wasn't mentally there for the sermons, however; I loved the way she'd rub my back and massage the football bruises out of my forearms as we quietly listened.

We dated for only five months before I decided to leave on a two-year proselytizing mission for the Mormon Church. I was assigned to serve in Scotland. A desire had arisen in me to tell others what I had found in my faith, but I was apprehensive about leaving. I was madly in love and knew Tamara was the one.

My fondest desire was that she would wait for two years until I got home, but I knew it was rare for young women to wait for their Mormon missionaries. Less than two percent actually do. And Tamara had the attention of all kinds of guys on campus. I knew they couldn't wait for me to leave so they could move in and sweep her away. I worried, but something deep inside me knew that what we had was real and would survive our separation.

While I was gone, Tamara and I wrote each other twice a week. We grew even closer through letters. There was something magical about communicating soul-to-soul with only what we could scrawl down on a written page. It was like having our long walks on campus and talking, only now it was a week delayed by mail and we were forty-five hundred miles apart. I would draw her funny little pictures and sketches of my experiences, and reply to her love notes and inspiring poems. We'd pour out our hearts, each sharing our deepest feelings and describing what was happening in our lives. I knew she dated others while I was away, but it boosted my confidence even further knowing that despite all her freedom, she still chose me.

After those two years, we had actually grown closer than we may have been if we'd been physically together. For us, it was true: absence had made the heart grow fonder.

Shortly after my return from Scotland, Tamara and I were married. We picked up right where we had left off. We were so much in love and so happy. I was twenty-three and she was only twenty-one. Our hearts beat in unison. We laughed and cried together, and we always knew what the other was feeling. And of course, we shared the powerful, physical magnetism of young lovers. Making our bond official through marriage was the perfect next step.

I continued my education in advertising design, and Tamara was finishing her own degree and took a job teaching high school in Bountiful, Utah. She wasn't much older than some of the seniors there and almost meshed right in with the students. She worked hard to earn her degree quickly by loading up her class schedule and continuing that same routine through summer semesters.

I also worked hard to graduate as quickly as possible, and when I did, my career took off. I landed a good job at a credible advertising agency right out of school and consistently earned the accolades to advance my position and salary. Tamara and I bought our first home, and things fell into place for us.

Three years later, Spencer, our first child, was born. He was a magnificent mixture of his mother and me. He had my prominent nose and his mother's crystal-clear eyes. His personality, however, was uniquely his own. Six years later our second son came, Griffin. He was all boy. Tamara would laugh and say that he was just like me in miniature form. He had my darker hair and a thick little build, but inherited his mom's mischievous grin.

We sold our first home during the housing boom of the eighties and made enough money to build our dream house in the foothills. We had a fantastic view overlooking the valley and the Great Salt Lake. I loved being in the mountains. Deer would frequent the yard, and the air was clear and fresh.

Life was everything I had ever expected it to be and more. All those fantasies I had created as a boy about marriage and what family could be like had become my reality. Things had fallen together in a way that almost surprised me. I would often sit on our deck at night in awe, simply feeling grateful for everything. A gorgeous and talented wife, two healthy, handsome sons, and a well-paying career in a field I was passionate about. And, mostly, I was thankful for the love I felt every day that filled my heart with joy. What more could a guy like me ask for?

CHAPTER 4

IT WAS MARCH 1997. Spencer was seven, and Griffin just over a year old. Spencer was growing tall and thin like Tamara's side of the family. Griffin was still too young for us to know for sure, but his little body was much thicker than Spencer's, and he showed all the signs of becoming a future linebacker. Easter weekend was coming up, and we planned to drive to St. George, a popular Southern Utah destination, to visit Tamara's family for the holiday.

On the morning of our departure, as we got up and prepared to leave, Tamara mentioned a dream she'd had the night before. She had just gotten out of the shower and was drying her hair in front of the mirror. I came into the bathroom and grabbed the towel that hung on the hook near where Tamara stood. I was about to hop into the shower myself when she said, "I had the weirdest dream last night."

"Oh, what was that?" I stopped and looked at her, noticing an odd expression on her face as she glanced back at me in the mirror.

"I dreamed you were marrying someone else."

"What?"

My heart sunk and I felt a tinge of resentment as she said it. The hot steam from the shower turned to a chill on the back of my neck. I tightened the towel around my waist, hiking it up a bit higher on my body as if to hide from her comment and her gaze. That didn't make any sense. We loved each other deeply and were more excited about our lives together now than we had ever been. We'd been married for ten years. Our relationship had depth; it was loving, passionate, and still a lot of fun. We always shared everything, yet this was a strange conversation. I wondered if she was angry or jealous of someone, or if she was worried about something we hadn't discussed. I wanted more information.

"Why would you have a dream like that?"

"I don't know. You were marrying someone else," she repeated. "It was really weird."

I saw her contemplative expression as she continued to gaze at me in the mirror. I stepped away from the shower and grabbed her shoulders, turning her around, to look directly in her eyes.

"That's crazy," I said. "Is everything okay?"

"Yeah, I think so. It was strange."

She turned away, back to the mirror, and started drying her hair again.

"So what now?" I shouted over the hair dryer. "Am I going to be in trouble all day because you had some crazy dream?"

I put my hand on her back and turned her toward me again. She clicked off the hair dryer. I brushed back her bangs, which were still warm from the hot air, and kissed her. "Don't let a stupid dream bother you, okay? It's not going to ruin your day, is it?"

"No," she insisted. "That's what I can't understand about the whole thing. I was okay with it. There I was, watching you marry another woman, and I was at peace. In fact, I felt content. It was so strange."

I wasn't sure how to reply. "I didn't create that dream," I said. "You did, in your pretty head."

"I know," she said, sighing. "It was just a weird dream." She kissed me again. "Now get in the shower." She smirked, as her mood lightened and she smacked me on the bare back. "You've still got to pack the car so we can get moving."

As we drove to St. George, Spencer had his *Star Wars* toys all over the backseat, including a Darth Vader kite we planned to fly in the breezy spring

weather. It was about a four-hour drive, and the kids nodded off for naps when we were less than halfway there. Tamara and I talked and enjoyed our quiet time together.

Nothing had changed between us since college. We still had invigorating, intelligent conversations, and laughed at ourselves when they got too deep. We'd philosophize and discuss current events, but our chats always came back to the children and what we could do to create happy lives and good memories for all of us. We made a big deal of holidays. We incorporated traditions from our childhoods and usually spent holidays with extended family. On Christmas, nobody was allowed to open presents until the entire family was up. We rang a Christmas bell signaling when it was okay to enter the room where Santa Claus and the elves had been.

Camcorders and cameras would capture all the joy as the kids entered the room. Halloween was equally festive. We'd carve traditional jack-o'-lanterns, and even the adults would put on costumes. Grandma Wendy would make beef stew, and the older cousins created a spook alley in the woods behind her house. Easter had its own traditions. We'd spend hours coloring eggs the night before and usually created a treasure hunt that led to big Easter baskets customized for each child. This upcoming Easter in St. George would be no different.

We arrived just in time for dinner without mishap, except for Griffin getting a little motion sickness on the way and throwing up in the car. After dinner, Spencer and I even had time to fly his new Darth Vader kite before the sun went down. The wind was perfect and I could smell the fresh cut lawn we were standing on. Tamara took off her shoes and sat down on the grass, waving her toes over the fringe of the blades as she held Griffin in her lap. Spencer's laughter seemed to waltz with the warm breeze as I watched him beaming while the wind tugged at the kite. He held on tightly and kept smiling at me as the kite climbed higher and higher.

It was one of those moments that burned into my heart. Grandma Ruby brought a blanket from the house and now joined Tamara on the lawn as they chatted about the Easter meal they intended to make and how Grandpa was doing. The kids were too young to even comprehend the situation with their great-grandpa. Grandma Ruby visited him every day, but was relieved to finally have him in a home where the entire burden of his care was not on her.

Griffin kept climbing off from Tamara's lap, pointing at the kite, then climbing back and forth on and off the blanket, giggling. Spencer and I effortlessly got the kite higher and higher into the air. We'd flown kites many times before—we liked flying kites together—but this time was magical. We didn't even have to run. We simply held the kite up against the wind and away it went, steadily climbing higher and higher while Spencer laughed and shouted about how well he was flying it.

During our weekend, we went to visit Tamara's convalescent grandfather. He was staying in a care center, and we hadn't seen him since his Alzheimer's had gotten especially bad. We were told he wouldn't know who we were. He had lost the ability to recognize even close family members or carry on an intelligent conversation. Nonetheless, we went to see him.

When we got to the care center, he actually did recognize us and carried on almost as if he were well. He remembered our children, even their names, and we had a wonderful visit. He kept saying, "I can't believe they're ours," as he marveled at the boys playing on the bed in his small, quaint care center room. We all hugged him as we left, but he wanted to hold on to Griffin. Grandpa kept laughing as he kissed Griffin on his chubby little cheeks. Finally, we said good-bye and went to spend the night with Tamara's parents, who were staying in their condominium nearby.

That evening, we colored eggs with the kids. I think they ended up with more dye on themselves than on the eggs. Afterwards, we filled up the tub with hot water and bubbles and let them play in the water until they were tired. We said prayers and tucked them into bed. After the house was quiet, I went outside to hide the eggs and arrange the Easter baskets Tamara had put together. It was a peaceful night, and I could smell the warmth of spring in the air. The cool grass felt so good on my bare feet.

I couldn't wait to see how the boys would react when they saw what the Easter Bunny had brought them. Griffin got fun little baseball toys in his basket, and Spencer's basket was stuffed with the latest *Star Wars* action figures (the few he didn't already have). He loved collecting things like that and would lay them all out in specific order on his dresser until he had collected them all.

On Easter morning, our boys woke up joyfully and went out to hunt for the eggs. Griffin was crawling about, calling each bright-colored egg a ball. Spencer found his Easter basket up in a small tree and decided the action figures were far more entertaining than colored eggs.

That evening as we all sat down for Easter dinner, Griffin was crawling in and out of a floor-level cabinet, closing the door behind him so he could hide from us. He did it again and again, squealing with delight, waiting for us to call three or four times before he'd peek out, burst into laughter, and start the whole process over again.

Griffin was a fun and mischievous boy. We had gone to great lengths to get him here. Spencer had been such a joy that Tamara almost immediately wanted more children. She had a severe case of endometriosis, however, and had undergone a partial hysterectomy a few years after Spencer was born. After almost five years of trying, we sought medical assistance and went through the extensive process of in vitro fertilization before Tamara became pregnant with Griffin.

It was difficult for me, too. I wanted Spencer to have siblings as I did; I knew well the beauty of sibling bonds. I also wanted Tamara to have every desire her heart realized. Watching the woman I loved feel as if she was in any way without, left me with a longing as well. Having Griffin now in our family had been nothing short of a miracle and filled us with a sense of completeness.

He was always laughing and into everything, especially the things he wasn't supposed to be. But with all his mischievous playfulness, Griffin had a tender side as well. He and I would play on the floor together at night before he'd be ready to get into his crib. I'd lie on my back and lift him high into the air. He'd spread out his arms as if he were flying. When he'd had enough, he'd lie down on top of me with his head right over my heart. He'd lay there like that for a long time until I thought he was asleep, but as soon as I'd move, even the slightest bit, his little head would pop up and he'd give me his silly "I fooled you" smile, then nuzzle his face back into my neck.

Griffin would wait for me at the top of the stairs when I'd come home from work. He'd sit there waiting and then yell, "Dad!" as soon as I'd come through the door. Then he'd start crawling in circles as fast as he could and laugh. He would get so excited that he looked like a puppy chasing his tail.

He didn't sleep well at night, though. He was an extremely colicky baby. I was often up with him into the wee hours of the morning as he cried with bad stomach aches. I found that if I held him on his belly with his abdomen resting on the palm of my hand he would find relief. We spent many long nights wrestling with colic. In hindsight, it was such a blessing; those moments together, however stressful, were gifts. It's almost as if he knew what might transpire, and simply wanted to give me every opportunity to spend more time with him.

CHAPTER 5

O N THE MONDAY FOLLOWING our Easter celebration in St. George, it was time to return home. After we said our good-byes and loaded into the car, I was surprised when Tamara insisted that I wait while she returned to the house to say good-bye yet again. *Women,* I thought. *Is one good-bye not enough?*

I watched, however, as she ran back to the porch to not only hug, but kiss both her mother and father. When she was finally ready to go, we made a quick trip through town, stopping only to gas up the SUV and get cold drinks for the ride home. At last, we were on our way, zipping up the interstate with the cruise control set at seventy-five.

Tamara, in her customary way, made herself comfortable by reclining her seat back. She reached over and took hold of my hand. I liked the way her fingers felt on mine. They were small and soft, and she always laced her pinky around mine. I'm not sure why she held my hand that way, but she had done it from the first time we ever held hands in college. I liked it.

We'd been driving for about an hour. Tamara was sound asleep. I checked the rearview mirror to see Griffin also sleeping in his car seat. Spencer was playing with his new *Star Wars* action figures and seemed content.

It's funny what goes through your mind in those quiet moments along a lonely stretch of road. I thought about work and all that had to be done when I got home. I looked out the window and noticed how beautiful the scenery was. I looked around at my family again and experienced a moment of intense gratitude. We'd had a great weekend. My wife slept lovingly next to me, holding my hand, the same way she had always held my hand since our first date. She only ever held onto three fingers. I was not sure why, but here she was still holding onto me the same way she always had. My children were happy and healthy. We were so blessed.

Thankfulness sank in even deeper as I took quick peeks again at each of them. I noticed the details of how Spencer held his mouth while he played, making lightsaber noises. I noticed Griffin's earlobes, hands, and fingernails, and how long his eyelashes were as he slept. It's interesting how much one can experience in the brief, truly observant moments. I glanced back over at my wife, Tamara, and noticed the way her wedding ring had turned on her finger. The only sounds where the hum of the tires on the surface of the street and Spencer's brief outbursts of playful *Star Wars* noises. The occasional wind gust would come up against the window strong enough to wobble the car just a bit, focusing my attention back onto the road.

I was so lucky. My family was beautiful to me. It was almost too good to be true, and, in fact, Tamara often expressed a fear that something might happen to us. I was the one she was concerned about. She was always so emphatic that I be careful. She would wait up for me when I had to work late. She had this strange fear of losing me. Maybe that's why she held my hand all the time, even as we drove. Perhaps I should have kept both hands on the wheel.

I don't recall the exact details of the next few moments, and maybe I don't want to know. There were strong crosswinds that day and reports of a red pickup truck driving erratically through that stretch of freeway. I also may have dozed at the wheel and swerved off the road, but for whatever reason, our vehicle, traveling at seventy-five miles per hour, abruptly went off the shoulder of the freeway.

I felt the vibration of the speed bumps and heard the scratch of gravel as the SUV cut to the right. Tamara sat up, screamed, and reached for the steering wheel. I yanked it left, over-correcting; we flipped over and began rolling, not into the soft grass on the side of the road, but down the middle of the freeway on the solid asphalt. We rolled seven or eight times, with all the punishing force of a five-thousand-pound hunk of metal, before coming to a stop.

I've spent a thousand haunting hours wondering how I could have avoided it and still don't have any answers. Did I fall asleep? How does one live with that? Could enough regret ever be associated with the notion that I was responsible? No one will ever know the nightmares I've endured, nor the asking why and how, nor the begging to take back those few seconds before we swerved.

There's that "undo" stroke on the computer keyboard; you know, the one you use when you type the wrong letter or want to put something back the way it was before. On my Mac, I simply hit Command+Z. How I wished they had that for real-life situations. I wished countless times that I could click a few buttons and make the whole accident reverse itself.

The car with my family in it finally came to a rest near an overpass by mile marker 80. As far as I could tell, I was on the floor under the steering wheel. I could smell the heat of the engine and the gasoline. I felt the sharp pricks of shattered glass all around me. I was in a daze, broken only by the sound of Spencer crying in the backseat. That jolted me into awareness. I tried to sit up but couldn't, and for some reason I could not see clearly. The warm sensation of blood was all over me. I had to get to Spencer. But if he was well enough to cry, I figured he must be okay.

"It's going to be okay, Son," I gasped, finding it hard to breathe. "It's going to be okay." I felt a ripping sensation in my midsection but didn't experience it as pain at first, only as the reality of my body being dismantled in some way. Perhaps it was adrenaline or simply the shock of what was happening. I could hear Spencer crying and pleading from the backseat, but I couldn't get to him or even adjust to see him. I was pinned in place, and it was the darkest kind of hell a man could ever know. The physical pain of my injuries began to swell in an indescribable way; however, the emotional torture was still so far beyond that. I told Spencer again it would be okay as

I lay there in a helpless, twisted heap, finding it almost impossible to speak or keep consciousness.

Then it hit me.

What about Tamara and Griffin?

Why could I not hear them?

Why wasn't Griffin crying in the backseat, too?

I lay there, still trying to grasp what had happened, and something in the core of my soul told me they were already gone. I felt it, more intensely than the pain of my physical injuries. Spencer's cries were screaming directly to my spirit, telling me the worst was true. I felt my wife and son's departures, not only in a physical way, but as an intense spiritual absence. They were gone. I felt them ripped away more keenly than the ripping pain in my stomach or the crushing pain in my chest and legs. The reality was overwhelming.

How can this possibly be real? I thought. Then I began to lose consciousness. As the world darkened, poignant thoughts came into my heart: *had I loved them enough?* Had I done enough? Had I been the father my boys deserved? Had I been the husband Tamara deserved? Had my life been worthwhile, and had I made a difference in any way? Thirty-three years . . . was that all I got? Was this the end?

I felt a breeze blow through the car as I began to fade. I heard Spencer again. It sounded like he was saying a prayer. I told myself I had to stay conscious. I couldn't imagine what my little seven-year-old boy must be experiencing. What was his view of what I could not see, being jammed on the floorboards like I was? I still had so much more to do, so much more to experience, so much more to love. Had I loved them enough? Had I loved them enough? That question kept pounding into my heart.

Even though it was broad daylight, I felt myself slipping into darkness—full of pain, regret, and guilt about what had happened to my family. The details of the day rushed through my head: how we got gas and soft drinks on our way out of town, and dropped off a video at the rental place. How the Saturday before, Spencer had wanted a kids' meal with a *Toy Story*

Woody doll, and the trip we took together to McDonald's to get one.

How Griffin had gotten motion sickness on the way down and we'd had to pull over. How it had felt to wipe his tender face and the little bibbed overalls he was wearing. It all seemed so important now that I was losing everything that mattered to me. Every detail came rushing through me with the horror of what had just happened.

The darkness was smothering me, yet I felt I had to stay coherent for Spencer. *I have to get to him somehow.* That was my last conscious thought. I struggled to breathe, spitting blood and feeling the tearing pains in my body. I heard voices, then sirens, and then I slipped calmly away into blackness.

I was gone from the scene of the accident, which was the most chaotic hell I would ever know, and had slipped from the nightmare into the quietness of pure nothing. Bright-white light encircled me, which seemed to be energized with pure, unconditional love. Peace infused this almost tangible light that now surrounded me. I realized, then, that all the pain was gone.

I was not aware of anything beyond a few feet around me, but I knew I was in a different place. This was a place of joy. It was familiar. It was home. It felt real, but I was not injured. I was not a floating orb or ethereal energy; I was myself. The same as I had always been, only now bathed in this familiar and amazing light. My natural senses were magnified to a greater degree. There were a million questions racing through my head, but as soon as I focused on one, its answer was immediately there. There was an ancient awareness, as if I had always been in this place.

I closed my eyes and took a deep breath, experimenting. There was no pain in my chest. I took another and became even more aware, as if waking up from a dream. Then I felt a familiar touch. When I opened my eyes, Tamara was right next to me. She was real, too; I could feel her. She was alive. I could feel her familiar vibration even more powerfully than her physical presence.

She looked the same as she always had, beautiful, but now I could feel her presence at a deeper level than ever before. Beyond how she looked, I was experiencing everything about the essence and power of her soul.

However, she was crying and upset.

Why were we here?

Was the crash a bad dream, or had I died?

Had we both died?

And where were the boys?

I had read about experiences like I was having. Many people described passing through a tunnel toward a bright light, but that wasn't happening to me. I felt like I was in some kind of protective bubble of light, with no tunnel or traveling at all. It was as if the light came to me. And I felt alive, not dead. I felt more alive than ever before. What was happening?

"You can't stay here," Tamara said with a voice that cracked with both urgency and sorrow.

"You have to go back. You can't be here."

Why was she crying?

"You can't come. You cannot stay here."

What did she mean I couldn't stay? I belonged here with her.

"You have to go!"

She was as real as ever. The thought of our boys raced through my head. Where were they? Were they here, too? If I stayed with Tamara, would Spencer be left orphaned? And where was Griffin?

"You have to go!" Tamara insisted. "You can't come. You have to go back."

But I didn't want to go anywhere. It seemed odd to me that in this glorious bubble she would be upset. Was it Heaven? I didn't know, but it made my earthly existence seem like a foggy dream. What I was experiencing was far more real, far more tangible, and far more alive than anything I had ever known. I pulled Tamara to me tightly. She was tangible as well. I even felt her wet tears on my skin. I kissed her. That was real. I smelled her hair. Not in the earthly sense, but with senses that seemed to be magnified tenfold.

"You can't be here. You have to go," she sobbed.

It almost felt as if my course was set. I didn't want to go, but I also knew she was right; I was not meant to stay. I felt I had a choice, but something deep within me knew I had to get back to Spencer. I had a little seven-year-old boy in the backseat of that crashed car. I felt like a contestant on a cosmic game show who knew the final answer, but wanted to quickly review every possible option, just to make sure, before the buzzer went off.

I looked into Tamara's eyes, those crystal, sky-blue eyes. Everything in the universe was calling me back to Spencer, but I wanted to stay with her. And where was Griffin? I felt a warm tear from her eye land on my face and roll slowly over my upper lip.

"I have to go," she said.

"I know." I heard myself say with hesitant conviction as the reality of going back sunk deep into the knowledge of my being.

I looked at her one more time, the love of my life, and the wife of my dreams. I leaned forward, putting my forehead on hers. Another tear fell from my eye and onto her eyelashes. I watched as it rolled down over her collarbone.

"I love you."

"I know."

I'm not sure I consciously made any effort to leave. I believe I would have stayed there with her, if not for the haunting reality of Spencer crying in the backseat of our crashed vehicle. I knew he deserved to have me there with him. He couldn't have every member of his family taken away in a blink.

My thoughts rushed to Spencer, his little-boy hands and long, thin fingers. The way the rooster tail in his flaxen hair bounced as he ran, danced, and played. I thought of the time a few years ago when we had sat on the back patio and shared licorice whips. I remembered that day. I could feel it, smell it, and taste it all again. The fresh-cut grass, the rhythmic sounds from the sprinklers and the sweet taste of the licorice. It all came rushing back. Most powerful was the feeling of my little boy right there with me watching the sunset. I had to get back to him.

As smoothly as I had ascended to that place of peace, I was away again. It had only been a brief peek into something profound, and as I drifted away, there was only one overwhelming question, not asked by a voice, but with energy that echoed into every cell of my being: "To what degree have you learned to love?"

CHAPTER 6

I N THE TIME IT took to draw my next breath, I found myself walking, or
at least moving at will, but in a very different place. The bubble of light
was gone. I felt the hustle and unrest of a ER trauma unit as I made my
way through the hallways of a hospital. I watched the doctors and nurses as
they went about their duties. I moved with ease all around them, still with
no pain at all. I suddenly realized none of them were aware of me. They
could not see me, but, *wow*, could I see them!

My perceptions were expanded. I knew each person I saw perfectly.
I knew their joys and their sorrows. I knew their love, their hate, their
pain, and their secrets. I knew every detail about them, every motivation,
and every outcome. I knew every emotion they were feeling, and I knew
intuitively why they were feeling it. In an instant, with no contemplation, I
knew them as well as I knew myself. I knew their hearts.

I looked into the face of a woman in her early thirties as she leaned into
a computer monitor at the nurses station. Although she appeared consumed
by her work, I felt her elation at the anticipated marriage proposal from her
boyfriend. I instantly knew that this was the second time around for her,
but also that this was Mr. Right.

I watched as a man in his late forties approached me. I felt his guilt over
words he'd had with his brother. I saw how his pride would never allow him

to take it back or apologize and how that disjointed him spiritually. He was literally splitting in two between remorse and arrogance.

I moved back into the hallway as another woman walked toward me from the opposite direction. She quickly looked down as she passed. It was almost as if she saw me. I experienced her pain from the abuse she had received as a child. I saw how broken it made her feel. I felt how damaged and unworthy she viewed herself and had for years. At the same time, I also felt her capacity to love and the strength she possessed because of what she had been through. I saw how her compassion was being drowned by her shame.

Just then, a young, heavy man in scrubs passed near me as well. He couldn't have been more than in his mid-twenties. I felt his self-loathing because of his obesity. As he awkwardly brushed past me and down the hallway, I saw the magnificence of his spirit. He was feeding his loneliness with food, yet he was brilliant.

I stepped aside, out of the hallway and into a room where I encountered a family. Someone had been shot or stabbed in violence. I felt their fear and anguish. I experienced the horror of the mother and anger of the father over what had happened to their son. I didn't merely witness it; I felt it within me. I was connected to all of them and their emotions as if they were me.

I left that scene and moved freely down the hallways and into other rooms. I encountered many more people, and I felt spontaneous, intense love for each and every one of them. Not a romantic love, but a perfect, compassionate love. My feelings were at a much deeper level than I had ever experienced before.

I moved about the hospital with ease, pausing to take in the beauty of the people I was encountering. I felt their true essence and marveled at the connection I had to each of them, even though I had never met them before.

I wondered about what I was experiencing. What if I could actually live my life with that same knowledge and connect with everyone I encountered at this level? What if I could feel every person's hurt and joy, and know every motivation for his or her every action or thought? What if I could feel the unconditional love I was now experiencing for every soul? I marveled at my perceptions. Most of my life I had actually avoided people. Now, everyone I saw was truly my brother or sister. In fact, it went even deeper than that. They were, in a strange sense, *me*! We were all connected pieces in a huge puzzle of oneness.

Words Jesus had said from my Christian upbringing rushed to my recollection: "Inasmuch as ye have done it unto the least of these, ye have done it unto me." Was he talking about the awareness I was experiencing? Did he feel the same thing I was feeling? Was this how he walked the earth, knowing each individual soul at this deep level of love?

I realized in a flash of inspiration that Jesus didn't see himself as better than the beggar or the prisoner; he knew he was one with them. He knew them perfectly, in the same way I was experiencing the strangers I saw now. We are all linked and equal in God's eyes. I was seeing it, feeling it, and experiencing it. They were me and I was them. I got the concept in a new, profound way.

After a while, I wandered into a room that felt a bit darker to me than the rest. There, I encountered some poor soul on a hospital bed, severely damaged. I didn't feel his emotions or perceive anything about him. He was a wreck of a body, a heap of seemingly-dead flesh.

I stood nearby, assessing the damage. It was so pitiful to look at, yet I felt no energy coming from the broken heap of a man. There was an intense sadness in my heart while looking at something so empty, so lifeless.

When I moved closer to look at the face of the man, I noticed the detail of his whiskers and how his sideburns fell along his ears. I looked at the mouth and nose, and that's when the realization hit me. I suddenly recognized who was lying there:

It was me! That was my body. I was standing there looking at myself, or more specifically, at the body I was no longer in. It seemed beyond repair, yet intuitively I knew I had to get back into it. I knew I had to return into that busted mass and be present with all the pain, guilt, and grief that would go with it.

As I looked at what had been me, another realization came flowing into my consciousness, almost like a tutorial and yet it felt like a remembering. I realized that my body truly was a temple. It was perfect in its form and its function. I really was created in the image of God. All of us are. I had a new appreciation for the perfect machine of my body I had always taken for granted. I never had to tell my heart to beat, my lungs to breathe, my eyes to see, or my ears to hear. I didn't even have to tell my feet to walk or my hands to work; they simply knew how. Yet here I was, witnessing my beautiful body in such a broken, pitiful state.

I reviewed in my mind biblical references I'd read surrounding our bodies being temples, except now I comprehended the meaning of such references in a whole new light. I realized that all the temples around the world, regardless of religion, are symbols of our bodies. I intuitively knew that any pilgrimage to a temple or Holy Place was representative of our souls entering into our bodies to receive enlightenment, an endowment, which is life. Life is what teaches us everything we came here to learn. Life is the gift, the rite of passage, the ordinance, the holy journey which truly expands the soul.

I also knew that any religious garment or ceremonial clothing, in whatever form or within any belief system, is symbolic of the glory which is ours by being clothed in our bodies. The body is the significant apparel symbolized by any of these religious or spiritual practices. Wearing the body throughout our lives, in sincere acknowledgment that we know we are more than just our flesh, plants us in a holy place continually.

All of this flowed to me with profound clarity in the brief moments I stood there as a spirit looking at my body. I knew in a very real way that I was not my flesh. However, I had a deeper appreciation for the flesh, which now was lying lifeless on the hospital gurney. I knew I was something far greater, far more eternal and far wiser than my body.

In that realization, I also had a profound sense of gratitude for the sacred gift which having this earthly experience in my human tabernacle offered me. I was out of the flesh, looking at my broken-down temple, my garment, my skin suit, my body, which I had removed from myself, or my soul. Only then did I realize the significance of what the gift of being "in the body" actually held.

Another insight flowed into my consciousness next. I knew in that instant that any baptism, sacrament, ordinance, or spiritual ceremony was symbolic of who we already are. All of those things simply point to what we are already doing as divine spirits, who have lowered ourselves into this realm to have a human experience. We are all born of God by coming here. We have all been blessed, washed, anointed, chosen, and clothed in glory simply by entering our bodies. No matter what gender, color, culture, height, weight, shape, or belief system, we are all the noble and great ones for having chosen to come and experience life in this realm. All of us glorious and divine simply by being here to play our part in the entire human experience. All of us perfectly connected to all of it.

I knew I was sent back to my life here for a reason. I had a son still living who needed me. Thoughts of Spencer rushed into my heart again. He was more than enough to live for, even in the broken condition I would now be in. Nothing is stronger than a parent's love for his or her child. I knew I had to move forward, even if life would never be the same.

As I stared at that body, the recollection of how that battered body had come to be lying there became real once more. I felt I was somewhere between heaven and hell. I had lost so much. I stood there looking at what was left of me. I had to get back into that broken heap and continue without my wife and youngest son. However, my oldest child lived. I knew that. He was probably somewhere in the same hospital. I could not allow him to be left orphaned. I took courage because I had to live for him.

As I made the spiritual commitment to enter back into my body, I actually remembered being born. I knew in a very personal way that I had been washed by the breaking of my mother's water. I had been anointed by blood during my birth process, and my eternal soul had been clothed in my glorious body to have my life experience. My birth was my own profound washing and anointing in a very real sense, as is everyone's who comes into this world. All the symbols pointed to a celebration of being born.

The last thing I remembered as I prepared to enter into my temple of flesh was another profound and powerful question. I didn't hear it in my ears, but in my heart. I was asked, "Who is the Lord's anointed?" I had always thought that it was someone special, higher than, or different from common humanity, but in that instance, my entire being knew the answer.

"Everyone!" I replied. "Everyone who has ever been born!"

And the voice echoed back, "Including you."

CHAPTER 7

I DON'T KNOW HOW IT happened. There was no struggle or movement. It was as quick as the mere thought of it. As soon as I consciously set the intention, I was there, back in my body.

But now, oh, the pain, both physical and emotional. The grief, the guilt, the burning, stabbing, pounding sensations all over my body. Wanting to breathe, to move, to speak. It was overwhelming, the heaviness and denseness of it. All of it was excruciating. I wanted to pull every tube from my arms, mouth, and nose and scream out. This could not all be real, but unfortunately it was. The thought of Spencer pressed on my mind. Where was my oldest son? How could I get to him? Was he okay?

Spencer had always been a great joy to me. He was the boy I had always dreamed of. He was a good baby, sleeping through the night at only three months old. He would play quietly by himself for hours, throwing balls or drawing pictures. He loved to wrestle and have tickle wars with his mom. He was kind and shy but brilliant in his own unique way.

He and I would lie for hours on the grass, looking at clouds, stars, birds, bugs, whatever interested us. As a baby, Spencer would sit across from me, and we'd roll a ball back and forth for hours. We'd scribble pictures and doodles and sketch on the floor together. He loved watching movies, usually the same one over and over again. We'd spread out a blanket on the living room floor in front of the TV, make popcorn, and create an event out of watching *Aladdin* or *The Little Mermaid* for the fourteenth time. He was my pride and joy. A father could not love a son more.

I had left him in the backseat of that car crying, and wherever he was, I knew he needed his dad. I couldn't feel him or sense him anywhere near me. My heart longed to see him.

As it turned out, Spencer was not in the same hospital with me at all. We had first been rushed to a hospital in Cedar City, but we had been immediately flown by Life Flight to two different locations in Salt Lake City: Spencer to Primary Children's Hospital and me to LDS Hospital.

When my family was notified of the accident, they divided into two groups. My older brother, Jed, and my mom went to Primary Children's to look after Spencer. My younger brother, Justin, and my dad came to LDS Hospital to be with me. When they first arrived at the hospital to meet me, Justin said I was battered so badly that he couldn't even recognize me when they brought me in. He said it looked as if every inch of my body had been beaten with a baseball bat. I was so swollen I looked like the Michelin Man.

Almost fifteen hours of surgery followed, with doctors working frantically to piece me back together. Both my legs had been badly shattered from the knees down. My rib cage had been crushed, collapsing my lungs. My right shoulder was severely torn out through the rotator cuff and deeply lacerated through my underarm. My left shoulder was injured as well, with a severe AC joint separation. The seat belt had cut through my midsection and lower abdomen, rupturing my intestines, which spilled out into my other open wounds and would become the cause for severe infections later on. I had a long gash through my left hip, actually exposing my femoral artery but by some miracle not severing it.

Oddly enough, I had no head injuries. The doctors explained that it was actually typical for athletes, particularly football players, to instinctively roll their shoulders and protect their heads. I had obviously done so, sacrificing both of my shoulders for the preservation of my head.

I couldn't comprehend much beyond the pain and grief I was going through. All the medical devices made it impossible to be at peace.

It was all a horrible blur, but I do recall Justin leaning into my ear and asking if I knew about Tamara and Griffin. "They didn't make it," he said. His tears fell on my own as I nodded, acknowledging that I knew. "Spencer is okay. He's in Primary Children's with Jed and Mom." I sighed with relief knowing my oldest son was all right and in good hands.

Spencer was actually released after a few days, with a broken arm and bruised ribs. I can't imagine what his young seven-year-old soul must have felt, after all he had endured. The emotional trauma and scarring must have ripped at him in even more powerful ways than it devastated me.

My injuries were severe, yet no physical pain could even come close to the emotional pain of knowing half my family had been killed. I could not escape those tortured, guilty thoughts, not even with all the morphine.

The only distraction from the emotional grief was the gripping agony that would come in waves from the physical injuries. On top of the pain was the discomfort from all the machines and medical devices invading my body to keep me alive. I hated it. I ripped at the equipment so incessantly in spite of my arm injuries that they had to tie down my left arm so I wouldn't tear out the needles and tubes. My right arm was basically immobile already, however I did have use of my right hand.

The respirator was the worst part, with the vacuum-like hose stuffed down my throat, forcing my lungs to draw artificial breath. It was so uncomfortable. I hated the creepy, artificial state of being; the feeding tubes, the traction, the restraints on my wrists. It was unbelievable. I kept wondering when I might wake up from the nightmare, but it never happened.

The only movement I had of my own free will was to use my thumb to press the handheld button for self-administering morphine into my IV line. I hate to admit it, but I used the morphine more for emotional escape than anything else. Every second was pure torture.

I was haunted by the notion that it was all my fault. I was driving the car. Had I fallen asleep at the wheel? Did I overcorrect in some drastic fashion? Maybe I shouldn't have set the cruise control? Or should I not have been holding Tamara's hand?

Overwhelming waves of guilt buried me almost every waking minute. How could I have avoided all this? Countless times I'd go over all the what-ifs in my head. I dreaded facing Tamara's family. Would they blame me for this? What would I say when I saw them?

I was finally conscious, but still heavily medicated when Tamara's parents came to see me. As I laid in the barred, cell-like hospital bed in the tiny clinical room, I could hear the voices of family in the hallway over the commotion of the busy nurses and staff. I immediately recognized the deep voice of Tamara's father. I was ventilated so I couldn't say a word. When the door opened, I sobbed uncontrollably. I was so worried they would hold me responsible. I was holding myself responsible. Why wouldn't everyone else?

Tamara's mother peered in, but stayed near the door. She seemed shocked and frightened to see my condition. Tamara's father came into the room, and it was a moment of pure truth. He's a big man, six-foot-five, and I had all the respect in the world for him. I didn't know how he would react, but as soon as our eyes met he simply rushed to my side and did his best, among all the tubes and medical machines, to hug me. We cried. I don't even remember if anything was said. I felt his pain, and it seemed as intense as my own. I didn't feel any blame at all coming from him; only love and empathy.

He didn't stay long. I really don't think we could bear the pain in each other's eyes. But his embrace was enough to give me comfort. He was more than a father-in-law; he had become a friend.

He left the room, and I continued to weep. The sorrow was simply overwhelming. The tragedy had reached so far and had affected so many people. What was I to do with it all?

I should have taken comfort in knowing I had been there, on the other side, even if only for a few brief moments. At least I'd gotten to say good-bye to Tamara in a strange kind of way. Most people don't get that chance. But the bereavement still plucked at my heartstrings with every breath I struggled to take.

Time became an enemy. The seconds clicked by like hours, dragging each day out into an eternity. My only relief was in passing out of consciousness.

Yet even in my sleep I'd have nightmares with scenes from my childhood; Halloweens with haunted house visits, where there always seemed to be a hospital vignette that looked far more like a butcher shop, except in my dreams now I was the piece of meat on the table.

When I wasn't having nightmares, I was in and out of consciousness, in and out of reality, and perhaps even in and out of the spirit world. It was such a disparity of experiences. I'd have peace and clarity, but then I'd awaken to the disaster and to the excruciating pain. I was going from pure spiritual communication in one realm to the prison of the hospital bed in another. I was halfway between this world and the next almost continually.

I'd dream of conversations with Tamara, or perhaps I actually experienced crystal-clear communication with my deceased wife. From her, I knew exactly what to do about the funeral plans. I even knew what Tamara wanted me to do with all her clothes and personal things. I also saw myself at the end of it all. I knew that somehow, I would eventually heal. I saw myself standing with a black cane in my right hand, smiling back at myself as I looked on. This gave me some sense of hope that the nightmare might end. That I may someday stand and smile, but it seemed so distant and unrealistic given my current state. It was a contradictory rip tide of both hope and hopelessness. *Hopeful* because I may heal. *Hopeless* because of the mountain before me that I had no idea how to climb.

It was touch and go for weeks. No one was sure whether I was going to die or not. It was hard for the family to make the funeral plans, not knowing whether they would be burying me along with Tamara and Griffin.

After almost ten days, nurses came to move me out of the ICU. It was a huge relief when the respirator was removed. I may have had too much morphine at the time because when they came in to get me, I actually thought I was going home. Nothing could have been further from the truth. I didn't know about the problem with my insurance. LDS Hospital was not in my insurance network, so I was being transferred to the University of Utah Hospital.

When the ambulance transport crew arrived, they were horrified at my condition and refused to move me. Insurance representatives insisted, however, that I be moved because they would not continue to cover my expenses at LDS Hospital. A Life Flight crew was eventually brought in to move me the few miles to a different hospital. The move nearly ended my life. My condition was critical, and the transport made it worse.

I arrived at the University of Utah in so much pain I couldn't stand it. The emotional jolt of having to endure a second hospital situation was unthinkable. In my heavily medicated state, I had truly thought I was going home. I wasn't prepared for being wheeled back into another ICU.

The only bright spot was that, during the time the respirator had been removed, I was able to communicate briefly with family members and dear friends who had been there with me almost constantly.

There had been discussions about the funeral and burial plans for Tamara and Griffin. The family had to move forward with arrangements in spite of my precarious condition. Tamara's family wanted her to be buried in Escalante, her parents' hometown, which was several hours from Bountiful, where we lived.

But I wanted Tamara and Griffin to be buried close to Spencer and me. It might have been selfish, but I wanted them to be buried in Bountiful, a few minutes from our home. I also knew they should be buried together in the same casket. I knew Tamara wanted her baby boy right there in her arms. She had communicated that to me during those strange exits from my body when I seemed to have clear connection to the other realms.

With the respirator removed for that short time, I was able to communicate our desires, and the family agreed to honor them. It was a miracle that I was able to share how I felt as those decisions were being made. I explained all my intentions for the services with no one knowing for sure if my own funeral would soon follow.

My business partner assisted me in putting down a few thoughts for the service as well. He wrote as I wheezed out my feelings. He kindly put his own touches on it as I struggled to communicate, but he captured what I wanted to say.

"I thank you all for your love and support on behalf of our family, and especially for your prayers. I know they are working.

"This is a hard day for all of us, but I want each of you to know that I have felt comfort and peace. I am deeply wounded, but not broken. My conviction is firm and my faith in all the promises made to us as a family is unshaken. My love for Tamara, Griffin, and Spencer is as deep and as pure as a man can have. I know they knew how much I loved them every day we were together. Because of that, I have absolutely no regrets.

"I cherished every sacred moment we spent together. There was nothing left unsaid or undone. My last memory before they were taken is of Tamara holding my hand. That is a memory I will cling to forever.

"It seems like Tamara and Griffin spent most of their lives waiting for me. Tamara always did get her work done faster than I did. Now I pray they'll please wait a little longer. Dad will be home soon, and, Spencer, please wait for me, too. I will be back with you before you know it.

"Please know that Spencer and I will move forward. I know we won't be left on our own. God is with us, the Comforter is with us, and there are two perfect, beloved angels here to take care of us. They will make sure we get back home together as a family, where we will fall into each other's arms and forget all the pain and sorrow of today."

Even though I was able to spit out a message of comfort, I was breaking into a million pieces inside. I wanted to be strong for everyone else, to stand in a place of power and give them hope, but I was hurting so badly my broken heart could hardly take another beat.

I knew I wouldn't be attending the funeral because I'd be in another ICU fighting for my own life. I ached, thinking of Spencer and what he must have been going through, all of it at the tender age of seven, and without his dad to comfort him during the funeral and all the events that were taking place.

My condition was bad enough that they hadn't let him see me yet. My open stomach wounds were grotesque, and the smell of my rotting, gangrenous leg filled the room with the stench of dead flesh. The injuries had been left open to allow air to fight the infection. The many tubes stuck into my body and the massive swelling made me nearly unrecognizable. It was best for Spencer not to see me that way. He knew I was alive and fighting to get well. That was enough.

He was living with my brother, so I knew he was in good hands, but the burdens he carried during that time must have been immense for a little boy.

CHAPTER 8

As THEY WHEELED MY gurney into the new hospital and began to make arrangements for my care, I could feel myself slipping. All that darkness was closing in on me for a second time. I passed in and out of consciousness. I could hear my mother begging me to hang on, and my brother trying to get the nurse's assistance. I began to vomit violently.

It was almost as if I was watching the whole scene from another dimension. Then the grief of the emotional loss hit me again, deeper than ever. It felt like pure panic, and I wanted in the worst way to get out from under it all. I'd had enough. At my core, I simply could not take any more. The despair felt like a lead blanket of blackness over my soul.

How could God allow this to happen to me? How could a God whom I believed was a loving father put me, or anyone, through such an ordeal? I knew at some level that others had gone through worse, but the sting of what I was experiencing was exquisite, and I could find no escape, no comfort. I had attempted to turn to God through silent prayers, but God didn't appear to be home.

I was still in and out of consciousness. My mind was in a constant argument between faith, knowing there must be purpose in this somehow, and blaming myself for the crash. I carried the intense guilt of having caused the death of two of my family members, along with maiming myself beyond repair. And then there was Spencer. I had broken his heart into so many pieces we could never find them, let alone put them back together again. It felt like the only reprieve from the intense waves of emotions was to escape into the numbness of the morphine.

I had always thought I was such a tough guy. I had learned to handle physical pain: working on the farm, riding bucking horses, training with the wrestling team, and bearing the impact of football. But those pains were nothing compared to this. The emotional grief was indescribable. They had buried my wife and baby, and I hadn't even been there. I felt so empty, so alone. Had they abandoned me, or had I abandoned them in some way? It was as if half my body had been cut off and left somewhere, and I couldn't find it.

As I lay there agonizing, delirious from the narcotics that didn't seem to touch the pain but only dulled my senses to the point of not caring how I felt, I actually had a demented idea about how I could put a stop to it all. In hindsight, I see how unrealistic it may have been, but it seemed so feasible in that moment. It occurred to me that in spite of my fighting it, I was probably going to die. I simply wasn't dying fast enough. The pain was so intense, emotionally and physically, that I decided a quick death would be the best way out.

I longed for that light bubble I had been in and the feeling I'd had there at the time of the accident. I also yearned to be with my wife again. I had already tried to escape through the excessive self-injections of morphine, hitting that button continually until I passed out. But I would always wake up again to the same pain, anguish, and nightmare. What if I could simply not wake up?

I believed if I could talk to my brothers, they would assist me in escaping. Jed was a cop and owned many guns. Maybe he would help me end it all, or at least bring me the gun and let me do it myself. If I could press that morphine button with the thumb on my one good hand, I could surely find a way to pull a trigger.

But Jed was so steadfast, so right. He would never put up with an easy way out like that. He had too much grit and would think of me as weak.

My younger brother, Justin would do it for me, I decided. He had the same moral fiber as Jed, but he had always been so close to me. We played football together in high school and college. We were roommates, and he knew me so well. I could convince him this was best. I had to try, and it was his turn for hospital duty. He was right there in my room.

My mind had gone a bit crazy. The idea was so far-fetched but somehow, I thought I could pull it off. I beckoned Justin close and explained my plan.

"I've got to end all this," I said to him. "I can't take it anymore. I have a plan, but I need your help."

Justin looked at me intently.

"I need you to sneak a gun in here." My voice was even and serious as I spoke. "It should be easy; there is little to no security. You can just slide it in the bed. No one would even notice. That's all I need you to do. Just get a loaded gun in here, and put it on my left side where my arm works. I can end this whole nightmare."

Justin pulled back and look at me in disgust and disbelief.

"I could finish off my already dying body, not to mention my soul. I'm done here. If you love me, you'll do this."

My pain and grief were too great. Even the feeling of responsibility for Spencer could not keep me there. My left leg now smelled so badly of rotting flesh that it stunk up the entire room. Gangrene was slowly destroying my body. In fact, my mother had been breaking open oranges and grapefruits that someone had brought into the room to try to hide the smell. I was literally going rotten right in front of everybody. I had to end it.

Why had I been sent back? Why couldn't I die? I'd lost my vision of being Spencer's dad. All that mattered was that I end the pain, and yet Justin refused. I couldn't understand why.

"Please!" I screamed at him. "Get me a damn gun! I can't go on!"

I was so disappointed when he rolled his eyes and yelled for a nurse. I begged and pleaded with him, but he didn't understand and continued to refuse me. He tried to calm me down as I became more and more angry. I could see the concern in his eyes.

"I think he's losing it, Mom." Justin looked to my mother who stood by the door, watching for nurses or doctors to come back in. I continued to scream at them both to get me a gun, and to get it now.

I began to vomit harsh, green bile again. The puking was so painful. The bile burned my throat and mouth as it came up: brown, green, putrid acid mixed with blood. I felt like I was on fire from the inside out.

The room began to close in on me as I tried to yell through the vomit. All the edges advanced toward me, as if I was looking at the room through a thick, round, glass portal. I became tiny lying on the bed, like a bug being observed through a magnifying glass. I looked down on myself. Everything focused in on me, yet I felt alone and small lying there on the hospital bed.

I continued to rise above the scene as my body got smaller and smaller. Everything was dark except my quivering body on the bed. It seemed like there was a spotlight on my convulsing physical form, which continued to become smaller as I rose higher above the entire scene.

I heard a hissing sound, and I was suddenly swept away from the horror of looking at myself to a more peaceful place, outside in the still night. I didn't hurt anymore, but I found myself observing an even darker scene. It was like I had broken through a time barrier and stood in a garden, but it was no heavenly place. I could feel despair coming from an isolated spot. There I saw a man shivering and convulsing in tremendous pain. I heard his pleas and whimpers as he asked for his cup to pass. I watched from a distance, but I could actually feel his anguish, and watched as he trembled and bled. I heard the words: "The Son of Man has descended beneath it all. Are you greater than He?"

I intimately understood the man's sorrow and grief. I could hear it, taste it, and feel it in the core of my soul. I shuddered. I was standing there, actually watching and feeling something awful, yet sacred. I wanted to rush to him. It was the same feeling I had experienced in the crash when I wanted to get to Spencer. I witnessed the suffering of this soul and knew I was not separated from it.

The feeling of being connected with everything and everyone rushed over me yet again. It was that same feeling I had experienced as I walked around the hospital shortly after the accident. I had an overwhelming sense of empathy. That's when the voice that spoke to my heart brought things to my remembrance again. I realized what I was witnessing was all about empathy. I knew I was not observing a price that needed to be paid to a judgmental God who demanded justice.

I wondered what loving father would punish one child to make recompense for what other children might do anyway? How could that be so? And what I was witnessing seemed to have nothing to do with that at all. This was about love, and knowing the emotions of the entire human experience. This magnificent soul was committed to literally feeling everything at its deepest level. Experience is the only way to truly know anything. This was not about sin, but about connection, pure empathy, and compassion. Otherwise, how would one know? And when one does know, judgments and comparisons simply seem to go away. Only love and compassion remain.

My consciousness raced back to my hospital room and into my body. Immediately I began to vomit violently again. However, something about what I had seen gave me a higher perspective. I now viewed my situation differently, and no longer felt so sorry for myself. My thoughts rushed to Spencer and why I was here. *I'm going to fight*, I decided in my head. I had been sent back, and the suffering I was experiencing was mine alone to bear.

Somehow, peace filled my soul. I laid my head back in pure surrender while finding renewed strength to do whatever was necessary to get well. I breathed deep and felt my pulse slow down. A new courage filled my heart; if Jesus knew on a very personal level what I was going through, and what it felt like for me, Jeffery, to lose my wife and son, then I was not alone.

He was totally familiar with my pain, in body and spirit. He had lost and suffered. He begged to have the bitter cup pass, and yet he accepted his life and his experiences with childlike meekness. I now had new perspective to do the same. Otherwise, I may be rejecting the very gift my life had to offer me. If experiencing was feeling, and feeling was knowing, and knowing was compassion, even divine compassion, then why would I deny myself that opportunity?

What if God's hand had played a part in my ordeal? What if there was a purpose in this madness? What if this was what I came here to earth to experience? Would this refine me and teach me things I could learn in no other way? The reality of these questions hit me. I'd been sent back to learn something. I too must rise again. I had the opportunity to be made more whole by what I was here to experience.

Gratitude began to fill my soul. Could I simply be thankful knowing this was a temporary experience, and I had deep lessons to learn from it? I was suddenly embraced by calmness that felt like a warm, soft blanket. I lay there, still quivering with pain but quiet in my heart. I was going to live! I would not leave my son orphaned. I felt deeper strength, love, and dignity. I was going to fight to live. The price to pay was mine. I had a renewed willingness to endure whatever it would take to heal. It was up to me, and a miracle, to overcome all of it and get well.

CHAPTER 9

LATER THAT NIGHT, A couple of doctors came in to tell me how sick I really was. They informed me that they were going to amputate my left leg above the knee. Not only that, they said, but I would also need several additional surgeries to save my life. By that time the infections had taken over, and my temperature had raced up to 106 degrees.

The hospital required a signature for the amputation to take place. Since I was in no condition with all the morphine to sign the papers on my own, a family member would have to sign the release. The idea of amputating my left leg above the knee was devastating to my mother. She hesitated at the responsibility of signing the form. The doctors put it bluntly: they'd have to amputate that night or bury me that weekend. My two brothers bravely stepped up and signed the release together so the doctors could move forward with the surgery.

As painful as it may have been for them to give permission to amputate my leg, it was a necessary step to save my life. A few hours earlier, I had been hoping my brothers would assist me in taking my own life, and now they were signing the documents to save it for me. That's how my brothers had always been; in my worst moments, they worked together to bring about my highest good.

The demand for a gun was far from my thoughts now. I was filled with the courage to survive. I was willing to take on whatever might come and face it with the strength of my whole soul. I was committed to be there for my oldest son, my brothers, and my parents.

That night was long. Many painful tests and procedures were performed, including putting me back on a ventilator. I was conscious as they fed the big tube down my throat. It was an awful feeling, like being strangled. My brother Justin was there with me every step of the way. I remember having adrenaline rushes as we went through the difficult procedures. He coached and encouraged me through the painful angiogram and other tests. It felt like a flashback to our days playing football and working out in the weight room together. We pushed ourselves to the limit while encouraging and supporting each other all along the way.

Thoughts of us racing each other as children came to my mind. I could feel the exhilaration of the ground beneath my feet and the muscles in my calves exploding with every stride. I thought about when we played little league baseball. We'd practiced "throwing guys out at second" for hours so we could actually do it in the games. I remembered running through the fields, chasing cows on the farm, pushing myself through wind sprints, wrestling in the third period, and being down by one point with twenty-seven seconds left.

I thought about college football and how sore my legs used to get during summer two-a-days. From running up and down the stairs as children to hiking in the mountains as adults, these scenes played in my head like clips from our old home movie collection my mom used to project for us on the living room wall. All the memories of how I had used my body in this life seemed to be vivid, right in front of my face.

Soon, however, they'd cut off my leg. All that would be gone, and only the old home movies would remain.

The projector in my mind stopped, and the film slowly burned up against the hot bulb of reality. I would be permanently dismembered, disabled for good. Would I ever run again? Would I even be able to walk normally? And would that even matter?

A new film started to play, but in my heart this time rather than in front of my face. Scenes of my lovely wife and beautiful children, happy family outings, and tender personal moments began projecting within me. The loss of my leg would never compare to losing Tamara and Griffin. My leg would eventually heal, but would my heart?

Before long, the amputation surgery was underway. I felt the burn of the general anesthetic going into my vein. It was a welcome escape from the hell of physical pain and emotional torture I was experiencing. *I don't care about the leg*, I thought. *Cut it off.* Nothing could hurt as bad as losing my family.

I watched the operating room lights go blurry and begin to fade. I thought I deserved this release from my reality. I wanted to revisit that place of peace. I even prayed in my heart that my soul would leave my broken body again, even if only for a short time so I could go back. I felt the ventilator fill my lungs with air one last time, and then everything went black.

When I regained consciousness, the physical pain was something I cannot even begin to describe. It felt as if I'd been unconscious for months. A fresh array of needles and tubes were now invading my body. Every cell throbbed with surges of deep agony. Not one part of my body was free from burning discomfort. I wanted to cry for help but couldn't. I felt trapped and caged. I was back in the ICU, but I couldn't find my morphine button. I had no relief, no escape from the torture. I couldn't believe it was real.

I eventually spent five months in the hospital, half of it in intensive care. The leg amputation turned out to be just the beginning. Over time I had eighteen surgeries, the most painful of which were the skin grafts. They harvested skin from my right thigh to rebuild my abdomen and hip areas. The days following that surgery were survived minute to minute. I was literally going from one breath to the next, simply dealing with the pain.

It's funny what races through your mind in those moments, hours, and weeks spent lying on your back trying to make sense of it all. Even with all the profound experiences I'd had, I found myself asking so many why questions:

Why me? Why now? Why did I lose both family members? Why did Spencer and I survive? Could we not all have gone together? Why did I have to be so banged up? If I had to go through this life without Tamara and Griffin, could I not at least be whole physically? Why did I have to lose my leg and possibly the use of my right arm? Why would God allow this? Why, why, *why*?

I eventually learned not to ask the why questions. There are no simple answers to such things. I had to discipline my mind to ask more "what" and "how" questions. What was I supposed to learn from all this? How could I apply what I learned to be a better person and a better father? How could I assist others?

Time continued to drag on for me. Each day seemed like a decade, and the nights were even longer, with so much pain, and uncertainty. I suppose if I hadn't been confined to a bed, I would have found ways to occupy myself and cope in a more productive manner.

But in my situation, I was too sick to read, let alone sit up. I was a prisoner in a hospital bed with no escape from my mind, nothing to take me away from the feelings that hurt so much. The only relief was the next surgery or the occasional few hours of sleep. I offered a silent, constant prayer for comfort and healing. I learned in those moments, however, that prayer had become a much different process for me.

Instead of doing so much asking and talking, I was learning to be still and listen. I was meditating, pondering, and visualizing more than pleading. In the past, prayer had been an active process, one of actually kneeling down and saying something, either aloud or quietly in a whisper. Now it was different. I couldn't kneel, nor could I speak, but I was finally communing. By being still and being willing to receive rather than thinking about what I might say, I found power, peace, and answers.

Slowly, one surgery after another, the doctors mended my body. Each time I experienced the escape of the general anesthesia, I hoped for another visit to that wonderful hereafter where I had been briefly before. I hoped for a chance to see Tamara or Griffin. But every time I went under, I only escaped to blackness and afterward returned to my new reality.

CHAPTER 10

I SPENT THE NEXT SEVERAL weeks in the I.C.U. in and out of consciousness. By now I lost the line that divided the two worlds we call here and there. I seemed to be in and out of my body continually. One foot was in this realm and one was in the next with everything in between blurred into a wide, grey area. The door to the other realms never seemed to close completely, either. It felt like I was in a void a lot of the time.

I would have never endured all the physical and emotional trauma without the love and support of my family. My brothers took turns looking after me. At least one of them was with me almost every day. They practically lost their jobs over the time they spent by my side. My mother would often sleep in the hospital room chair because she didn't want to leave me alone during the night.

My father would come in and sit for hours. I knew it was hard for him to see me so maimed. I had been his strong, healthy son, but now I was broken—both body and spirit—and he couldn't do anything. I could see the helplessness in his face. I was so grateful for his sacrifices. His quiet comfort and support assisted in my healing.

My business partners, extended family, and friends would each take their turns at my bedside as well. They will never fully realize how much their attention, time, and love meant to me. I was lucky to have so many people nearby who loved and cared about me. I've wondered what people must go through who have to suffer like that all by themselves.

As loved ones came into my hospital room, I begged for the removal of the ventilator. I would dream of taking a cool drink, or actually talking with my visitors instead of only being able to make gestures and scratch down notes.

Nurses would come in to move me and change my dressings, and while they heaved my broken body from side to side, I would beg them with gestures to remove the ventilator as well. My chest and abdominal ailments were so severe that I had actually forgotten about the amputation. The infections were terrible. My temperature fluctuated between 104 and 106 degrees. They put me on a special mattress filled with cold water to relieve my fever.

My lungs had gotten worse as well, mostly because of all the time I spent on my back. Pneumonia had become the norm for me. The amount of antibiotics they pumped through my body to fight it was shocking, but they had to try everything to get my lungs cleared.

Each morning, the X-ray crew would appear and lift me enough to slide the cold film pack under my back, and take yet another chest X-ray. At least the coldness of the pack against my burning body reminded me I was alive.

I kept pointing and complaining about my right arm. They had been working so diligently on my lower extremities and midsection that little attention had been paid to my arm. All I knew is that I could not move it and it felt numb, which worried me greatly. They had stitched up the laceration under my arm, which was healing, but the lack of movement and feeling in my shoulder was disturbing.

They discovered that the rotator cuff had been completely torn out and that not a single muscle was still attached in that area. Most of the nerves had been severed by the deep lacerations on the inner side of my upper bicep. They said I had been through so many mandatory, life-saving surgeries that my body would have to get stronger before they could do anything more for my shoulder and arm.

My muscles had begun to atrophy drastically. At that point, I had been immobile and on my back for nearly two and a half months. I was making progress; however, it was slow and with many setbacks. I was resolved at that point to get home. I was committed to healing no matter what it took. It was the spiritual courage that seemed to bring physical healing. I had resolved to expect miracles and asked my own spirit continually to heal my physical body in every way possible. I had spent enough time between the realms that I knew full well my spirit was whole. I simply wanted my body to follow suit and manifest health.

The day finally came when my lungs were well enough for the ventilator to be removed. I remember the relief and elation when they told me they would be taking it out. Of course, the other PICC lines, IVs, feeding tube, and catheters would remain, but I was finally well enough to breathe without the assistance of that dreadful machine.

It was a little frightening as they pulled the ventilator out of me, but it felt so good to be free of it. My big brother, Jed, was there as this happened. All my life Jed had kept me safe. I cried for a drink right away, wanting so badly to cool my throat. Jed and I finally convinced the nurse to give me a sip of water. It was heaven to swallow it, but it came right back up again. There wasn't anything in my stomach, so the small amount of water coming back up was no big deal, however here I was vomiting again. Would it ever stop?

My brother Jed assisted me to keep taking tiny sips until I could keep them down. After a while they let me try 7UP. Awesome is the best way to describe how that tasted. Oh, how I had waited for that moment. The way it tingled on my throat was incredible. To this day that is the best sip of anything I've ever tasted. However, moments after swallowing, like the water before, it came right back up and I began to dry heave. My system wasn't ready and couldn't take it.

My voice was raspy and weak, but talking to my brother was the best medicine I could have had. We even laughed that day as they tried to sit me up in an electric recliner because we noticed that the back of my head had been rubbed bald. We laughed about it. We actually laughed.

That was the first time I realized I was going to heal. In those moments, I knew that someday I would be done with the physical part of my ordeal. I was so thankful for my big brother and the time he had spent there with me. His spirit and strength were paramount to my recovery. I actually slept that night.

CHAPTER 11

THE NURSES AND HOSPITAL staff were kind and caring. On one particular night, as I lay awake in the darkness, a nurse came in and asked if I'd like to have my hair washed. It had been a hard night, and I felt like I was dying emotionally, wondering how and if it would ever end. All I could do was nod yes. He proceeded to quietly wash my hair. Tears streamed down my face as he used a small basin to do the best he could to catch the water as he cleaned my hair and face.

I don't know who the nurse was, and I never saw him again, but he was a ministering angel to me that night. There was something saintly and almost divine about his being. I have often wondered if it was a nurse or some kind of angel that came to my aid, offering that simple act of kindness in one of my darkest hours.

The nurses continued to change my dressings every day. Even after three months, the wound in my midsection was still open. They packed it with rolls of gauze daily to fight infection and improve healing. It was bizarre to have that huge opening in my stomach. Both of my brothers watched closely as nurses changed the dressings, learning how to pack the wounds themselves. It was extremely painful, and I often preferred to have one of my brothers do it rather than the nurses. My brothers knew my personality and could move through it in a manly, deliberate way despite my wincing. Doing it quickly and getting it over with was best even though it hurt.

On one occasion, we were having a tough time getting through it. My brother was coaching me through the process with forceful words. "Hold still! Stop wincing!" In the intense pain, I closed my eyes tightly. He continued to give me tough talk as we attempted to get the gaping wound packed properly. I opened my eyes to peek up at him while he was working on it and berating me with his tough guy talk, and I noticed he actually had tears streaming down his cheeks as he packed the open wounds of his brother.

I learned a lot about real men in those times. Toughness and tenderness must go hand in hand in order to be a true man. Men were meant to support and mentor each other rather than always compete. I wondered what the world would be like if all males joined with each other in brotherly love. We certainly wouldn't have wars anymore. Love would take precedence over always winning or having to be right.

I did prefer to have the nurses care for my colostomy. I was so embarrassed about it and found it gross to have a family member have to change me. The nurses would have taught me how to do it myself, but with only one working arm, it was too difficult for me to accomplish. I appreciated the assistance.

It was so humiliating for me, a grown man, to have everyone knowing when I went to the bathroom and having someone come change and clean the bag. The ruptured intestine would eventually be repaired and the colostomy taken down, but I had a lot more healing to do and more strength to gain before my body could take another major surgery.

I was on a first-name basis with almost all of the nurses by then. One day, a couple of young female nurses came in to give me a shave. They were kind and cheerful and made me laugh. It felt good to be in their company.

Many hospital staffers also spent time talking with me. Some engaged in deep, personal conversations. They told me things that bolstered my spirit when I needed to hear them most. I didn't have anything to hide from those folks. It gets pretty personal when someone is changing the dressings on your lower abdomen or dealing with your colostomy.

I kept a picture of my family by my bed. Often nurses would ask and listen while I talked about my wife and children. The staff members were as concerned about my soul as they were my body. It meant a lot to me that they cared.

Eventually I was well enough to receive more visitors. People from work and from the neighborhood joined family members in my room for regular visits. They were willing to do almost anything for me. One neighbor even scratched my foot for me since my stomach injuries prevented me from sitting up and I still didn't have the use of my right arm. Few things are worse than having an itch you can't scratch, and I appreciated her willingness to do that for me.

I was grateful to everyone for what they were willing to do on my behalf. I was so blessed. My brothers, family, and friends would still sit with me late into the night or even stay over to keep me company. I still didn't sleep much and sometimes wanted to talk. I learned that there is no greater power than family love.

On one particular afternoon, a couple whom I did not recognize came to visit. I was embarrassed at first, since I could not place them. It was a man and woman about my same age, nicely dressed and pleasant, yet I knew they weren't from my work or from my neighborhood. It was awkward not knowing what to say.

"Allow me to introduce ourselves," the woman cheerfully chimed in. "We are members of your first ER trauma team. I'm one of the nurses, and this is one of the doctors that saw to you when you were first life flighted into the hospital."

I was touched that they had enough compassion to come and see me at a different hospital, several weeks after the accident.

The doctor leaned against the wall at the other side of the room, while the nurse moved close to my hospital bed and kept talking with me.

"You look far better than when we first saw you."

"Yes. Thank you," I replied, not sure what to say.

"You have our deepest sympathies. We are aware that you lost your wife and one of your children in the accident."

"Yes. Thank you," I repeated, almost robotic as I simply wasn't sure why they had come and how they even had the time to do so. I was sure they had hundreds of patients and it felt strange to think they came to visit me.

"Are you comfortable enough and getting the care you deserve here?"

"Yes," I assured her. "They've been very good here."

I did not remember the doctor or nurse from the previous hospital. The spiritual things that happened remain forever fresh, but details of my care and the hospital staff I admit were a blur. We continued to make small talk for several minutes, the nurse doing most of the talking. I continued with my simple answers to her questions. The doctor looked on, saying very little, but was intensely involved as a spectator in the conversation.

Suddenly. the nurse stopped and became quiet. I saw tears begin to well up in her eyes. "We have to tell you why we actually came to see you."

She sat down on the chair by my bed and grabbed the box of tissues from the hospital tray. The tears were now flowing freely as she kept dapping her eyes with the tissue to keep her mascara from running.

"When they life flighted you into our facility, I was one of the first people to come into the room. As I did, I experienced an intense feeling of love, stronger than any I had ever felt before. As I looked at you, you seemed to be surrounded by light."

Her strong emotions had by now brought tears into my own eyes. I lay there silently with the tiny, wet streaks trickling down my cheeks as she continued.

"I saw the form of a woman standing by your badly damaged body. We knew you had lost your wife and one of your sons in the car crash . . . but I saw her, your wife, standing right there in the light that surrounded you."

My tears now ran freely, and I was speechless.

"I felt her love for you. I knew somehow that you were going to make it. I also felt her concern over you remaining here as she was on the other side. I felt her feelings so powerfully, and it has had a powerful effect on me. We simply felt it was important to share with you what happened."

I was so moved by what she was telling me that I now freely cried with her. If she had seen Tamara's spirit, then what I experienced after leaving the scene of the accident wasn't imagined. Tamara had been with me; it was real.

The nurse continued, "When I saw her, I was so overwhelmed that I ran to get the doctor." She wiped away her tears, and motioned to the doctor, still leaning against the counter on the other side of the room. He had been silent so far.

"I had an interesting experience as well," he added hesitantly. "Had I been more involved in your actual care, I may have been too focused to experience what I did, but I felt a strong presence of your wife as soon as I entered the room. I was quickly assessing your injuries from a high level while the other experts were actually working on you, but I could feel your wife. She was behind me. The feeling was so strong that I turned and I too saw her. She was actually communicating with me. Not in words necessarily, but I felt her say, 'thank you', and communicate in a powerful way her gratitude for all that was being done on my behalf."

The doctor stopped as if holding back from saying too much, but that's when I knew for sure they were telling me the truth. It was so much like Tamara to insist on thanking everyone. Even in a crisis, she would have been the first to show gratitude to the people who were assisting me in that critical moment.

"It's so good to see you improving and doing well," the nurse added again, breaking the awkward moment of silence. She wiped away her tears and gave me a big comforting smile. I still wasn't sure how to respond.

They didn't stay long after that. I thanked them for coming and told them how much it meant to me that they took the time to visit and share so openly.

"We may see you again," the doctor added as they waved and quietly shuffled out the door.

I thought long and hard about what they told me. It boosted my spirit to know that people around me had also experienced something significant at the time of the accident. What they felt was powerful enough that they took extra effort to come share it with me. Their stories brought not needed but much-appreciated validation to my own experience in many ways. I found peace in the fact that what had happened to us had affected even members of my medical team. To me, that was amazing.

We do live on; I knew it. Something is beyond the body and this life, something tangible and real. This experience wasn't just a Sunday School story anymore. It was a reality, and I had been there. I had peeked into the hereafter, if only for a moment. I had been to the other side and tasted that peace and joy. I had said good-bye to Tamara and members of my medical staff had felt a portion of it in some profound way.

I made great progress after that. I was actually healing and feeling much better. I was well enough that Spencer began making regular visits to see me. He would climb right up on the hospital bed with me and read books, talk, and tell stories, or watch basketball on TV. The Utah Jazz were playing the Chicago Bulls in the NBA Finals and we enjoyed cheering on the home team from my hospital bed.

Spencer made me a little beaded *Star Wars* bracelet he called my Force bracelet, so I would have courage and the Force with me. His infatuation with *Star Wars* made it easier to explain my broken body and missing leg to him.

"I am like Darth Vader," I explained. "And they will put me back together with cool robot parts so I can come home and be your dad again."

Spencer remained silent, looking at the bracelet he had beaded together as if in disbelief. And yet, what else could I expect? I wasn't sure I believed it either. So much had changed.

I always felt sad and empty when he left. I worried so much about him and how he was doing. He didn't want to talk about the wreck or our loss at all, only about when I would be coming home again. I realized I hadn't been there for him when he deserved my love most because I had been so sick for so long.

The family had gone through the grieving process and funeral while I was fighting for my life in the hospital. I was barely well enough physically to begin dealing with Spencer and how to get us through this ordeal. It had been over three months. Family members were beginning to move on emotionally, but I was *far* behind them. I was reliving the loss in a new way through Spencer.

I had a little box put together for Spencer. I asked my mother and sisters-in-law to go to the house and let him select some things that would remind him of his mom and little brother. He selected a scarf that Tamara had worn. It still smelled of her perfume. He also chose a necklace with animal charms on it. He selected a pair of Griffin's little shoes and a few family pictures. These tokens were all simple things, but they meant the world to him.

It broke my heart when he brought in the treasures he had gathered. Because of their injuries, Tamara and Griffin's funeral had a closed-casket, so Spencer never got to see them or say good-bye. He deserved closure in some way, and remembering them by saving little reminders of their lives, not their deaths, was extremely healing for my little boy.

Watching my son deal with all of it with such courage was inspiring and gave me great strength. He only cried once when he was with me, and I could tell he was doing his best to not make me cry, too. I continually fought to hold back the tears around him. The very sight of him both broke my heart and filled it with gratitude. I wondered how I would ever raise him alone. How could I make this right for him? How could I replace all he had lost and give him the kind of normal, happy childhood he deserved?

My heart was filled with gratitude every time he'd climb up on the hospital bed and lie close to me. He'd talk about school, his cousins, *Star Wars*—anything but the wreck. I knew he was avoiding it, and I avoided it too, for his sake, trusting that he had grieved in his own way while I had lain unconscious in the ICU. I didn't want my pain to tear open his wounds again. I felt that talking about it would bring it all back for him. He was healing; I was behind because of the time I had spent unconscious and trying to stay alive. It was difficult to know how to comfort him.

Having a child is like having your heart leave your body and walk around in the world. I wanted the best for him; I wanted him to heal emotionally. I just didn't know how to be there for him with my own heart still broken in so many ways.

CHAPTER 12

O VER THREE MONTHS HAD passed. The feeding tube had been removed. Only the IVs, oxygen tubes, colostomy, and a catheter were left to deal with. This was such a vast improvement over my earlier condition that I almost felt close to normal.

I was eventually moved from the ICU to surgical recovery, and finally to the rehab floor. It was there that I first saw myself in a mirror. I was quite a sight. My eyes were red and hemorrhaged. I had lost sixty-five pounds. There were scars all over my body, and the wound across my stomach was still open. My hair was long, except for the bald spot my pillow had worn off the back of my head. My whole countenance looked like death, even though people had been commenting for weeks on how good I looked. I felt as if I were looking at a stranger. The only thing I recognized was the pain and sadness in my eyes. That I knew well.

The nurses asked my family to bring in sweatpants and a t-shirt for me to wear in place of my hospital gown. They told me I would be going to the rehab gym to begin working on my badly atrophied body. I welcomed the idea of regular clothes until I actually tried to put them on. I immediately became acutely aware of how injured I still was. I gazed at my body, and the empty space where there'd once been a leg.

It felt so strange pulling on the sweatpants without putting a foot in first to feel my way through the pant leg. I also realized that my abdominal injuries were too severe for me to sit up properly. I still only had the use of one arm. It was such a struggle to get the sweatpants on that I collapsed back on the bed, my spirit broken for a moment. Justin saw my anguish and finished dressing me, then called the nurse to assist in transferring me into a wheelchair.

Justin, with the assistance of a male nurse, lifted me into the chair. I was too weak to do it myself. My brother pushed me down the hallway. My whole body jiggled in pain with every little bump. The muscle atrophy was unbelievable. I was like a skeleton wrapped in gelatin. This could not really be my body! I could not hold back the emotions.

"I'm a gimp!" I blurted out as Justin pushed me through an open doorway. "My wife is dead, my youngest son is dead, and I look and feel dead."

I was always close enough to Justin to talk to him that honestly. He was younger than I was but had become one of my wisest counselors. I trusted him with everything, even when I was frustrated and overwhelmed. The wheelchair ride that was meant to raise my spirits had instead provided a brutal shock as to what the reality of life had become.

I threw up again, and he took me back into the hospital bed to rest. I rolled over and let myself break inside. I did not have the strength to do anything else.

I slept that night but had a crazy dream. All night long I dreamed that I was trying to call Tamara. I called our home phone over and over again but got no answer. I called her office phone at school, but it just rang. I called her parents' phone and got an answer, but they told me she was not there. I was trying to remember her apartment phone number from way back when we were in college to see if she might pick up that call.

It was the worst nightmare. I dreamed all night of trying to find her, calling every number we had ever had and all of her family and friends' numbers to see if I could speak to her. When I finally woke up the next morning, the sun was already blazing into my hospital room. It felt warm on the white sheets of my bed. I wondered who had opened the curtains for me and let the sun come in. It was a welcome change from the dreams of the night.

The days continued, each one offering new challenges and realities, but I was healing. Every day I got a little stronger. The oxygen mask was finally removed. Only the colostomy, PICC line, and catheter remained. I started to enjoy the short trips to the rehab gym to move what remained of my limbs. The exercise felt great, even if I was simply raising the stump of my amputated leg or lifting a small weight with my one good arm. I even broke a sweat at one point. Wow, sweating in a gym—now that felt good, and almost normal.

The nurse and physical therapist brought me back to my room and assisted me into the shower. Yes, shower! It was the first cleaning I'd had outside of a sponge bath for months. The hot water felt wonderful as I sat in the shower chair and let it run down my back. The nurse helped me dry off and offered to cut my hair, an offer I gladly accepted. She also trimmed my fingernails, which had become quite long. I felt like a new man. I even ate dinner that evening without puking.

Coworkers and business partners from my office came to see me that night. I told them about the visit I'd had from the ER doctors earlier that month. I hadn't talked that much in such a long time. I realized how hard carrying on a conversation was without losing my breath. It was strange and something I hadn't noticed before. When my breathing became more difficult, I mentioned the problem to the nurse. When my vitals were checked, I was put back on oxygen immediately.

Things got progressively worse late that night, and I began to feel very sick. Nurses took me to radiology for another look at my lungs and then rushed me from the rehab floor back up to intensive care. Doctors scurried about and then explained to me that I had not one, but two pulmonary embolisms, or blood clots, which had lodged in my lungs. I had battled pneumonia for months, and now this. My lungs were still damaged from the trauma of the accident, and the blood clots were not helping. I could tell from the look on the doctors' and nurses' faces that it was serious.

I felt progressively sicker and quickly began to fade again into that semiconscious state of delirium. The *why* questions started bombarding my head again: *why this now?* I'd been getting better. An interesting thing began to happen as I rolled back into the delirious state. I suddenly felt the souls of the people working on me in that same, intense way I had right after the crash.

I could feel each person's energy as he or she came into the room, but I was very much in my body this time, and the pain and sickness were overwhelming. I was scared because it had escalated so quickly. I felt myself slipping into that darkness again, but the doctors' worry and concern were still prominent in my mind. It was strange to be so aware of their feelings.

Encountering people's spirits this time was interesting; it reemphasized what I had experienced before. I felt and recognized each beautiful soul as they continued my care over the next few days. Some of the most wonderful spirits were not necessarily the most attractive people. I learned not to look on someone's appearance but instead to feel his or her soul. I found myself closing my eyes as the doctors or nurses entered the room to feel who they really were. Experiencing someone beyond how they look is a profound experience. Even now I often close my eyes to recognize the character of someone's soul beyond what he or she looks like.

I stabilized after a few days. I was put back on oxygen and blood thinners, but apparently, I had cheated death yet again. It was awful to feel so sick, however; I could not eat, and a feeding tube was re-inserted. I hated the feeling of it running down through my nose and into my throat. At least I didn't have the respirator this time around. Somehow the oxygen tubes through my nose were keeping enough air in my lungs. I continued to try to move in bed as best I could. I didn't want to lose the ground I had gained in tightening up what muscle I had left.

I began to believe I really couldn't be killed. After everything I had been through, my heart kept beating, and my damaged lungs continued to draw breath. Even when I had wanted to die, my body wouldn't quit. At that point, after overcoming the blood clots, I knew I was definitely on earth to stay.

During this time, I received a visit from my high school football coach. He had moved to California shortly after my senior year but had heard about the accident and flew into Salt Lake to see me. He had been an all-American collegiate player and also played in the NFL.

I was inspired by his visit. I had not seen him since I was eighteen years old, fifteen years earlier. We had been close when I was in high school, and his visit gave me a well-deserved boost. I was moved that he would fly clear to Salt Lake to see me, as well as the fact that I was even on his radar after so many years.

As we talked, he removed his all-American collegiate ring and placed it on my finger. I had lost so much weight that it dwarfed my thin and badly atrophied hand. I told him I could not accept such a gift.

"I don't want you to keep it," he said, looking me in the eye. "But I'll only accept it back when you can stand up, walk to me, and return it like a man."

I was shocked into silence, unable to speak. My gaze kept going back to the heavy ring on my finger.

"I know what you're made of, Jeff," he told me. "Rehabilitation is going to be hard."

I knew very well that learning to walk again would be a challenge, not to mention overcoming my other injuries. He cried at my loss and what I had been through but motivated me to continue the fight and get back to full health. It was time for me to get back-to-back to my life. Not only for my son but also for me. It may have been the greatest halftime speech he ever gave. Since his large ring did not fit my finger, I wore it on a leather strap around my neck. It was a great motivator, inspiring me to heal.

I eventually gained enough strength to be moved back to the rehab floor and continue my recovery. I returned to the hospital gym daily. I worked at standing on my one good leg, not that it was "good" considering that I still had six pins and a metal plate holding it together. Despite it all, being upright on my foot, even with assistance from the nurses and stabilizing bars, was an amazing feeling.

Time moved on. I began to enjoy my wheelchair rides with my brothers, family, and especially Spencer. We'd go outside the hospital for short jaunts. I had worked hard and was almost well enough to undergo my last few surgeries. Most of the tubes were gone by now with the exception of the PICC line and the colostomy bag. I would still breathe oxygen while resting in bed but was no longer required to wear the mask full-time. The catheter had even been taken out, and I cannot describe how wonderful it was to relieve myself normally. The pneumonia was diminishing, and I was getting stronger every day.

Family and friends were allowed to bring in outside food from time to time. I needed all the calories I could possibly consume for healing. Milkshakes were a regular indulgence in the evening, and I was actually keeping things down. I loved it when they would bring me sushi. I even got to the point where a big pastrami burger sounded good and I could eat the whole thing. By then I was up to a whopping one hundred sixty pounds, still fifty pounds lighter than my natural weight, but I was recovering.

Hospital staff would come in and marvel at how well I was doing. They all said they could not believe I was alive. I was a living miracle. Doctors came in each morning to chat and check my wounds. They brought in counselors who told me I would grieve the loss of my limb for a while, but they had no idea how I was grieving the loss of my wife and son. I constantly battled to keep the depression at bay. I could not speak of them without falling apart. Though I was winning my physical battle, my emotional war still raged.

I knew I had experienced something beyond death, but it didn't quench the pain of missing them. I would dream of Tamara and Griffin often, only to wake and find them still permanently absent. I read books, prayed, and did anything to find comfort. I would even tell myself that it was all temporary and that someday, they would be safely back in my arms again. But it didn't take away the loneliness of the present.

I was in the hospital gym one day for my regular rehab routine when I encountered a young man in a wheelchair who looked about my age. He seemed familiar in a way, but I blew it off and continued my mild workout. I thought it odd that standing up on one leg for brief moments or lifting a two-pound weight could be classified as working out.

As I thought about the irony of it all, the young man approached me and said, "I think I know you. Did you play football at Wasatch High School?"

I answered that I did and he explained that he had played for Park City High, a nearby rival. He recalled that we had opposed each other in a hard-fought game sixteen years earlier. We had both been named to the All-State team, and he remembered who I was. Strange, that after all these years he would recognize me and yet as my memory rolled back, putting things into context, I absolutely remembered him and why he had seemed so familiar when I first saw him.

Of course, he also took great joy in reminding me that his team had beat us by three points in the last few seconds of that game. Yes, I remembered that too, even if I'd rather have forgotten. What a predicament we now found ourselves in, two All-State football players, both in wheelchairs. Unlike him, however, I was able to stand briefly, even if it was only on one leg. We talked and even laughed about our situations.

He explained that he had also been in an auto accident, which had broken his spinal cord, leaving him a paraplegic. He envied that I could move my legs even if one of them was only a stump. I became melancholy as I shared with him how I had also lost my wife and youngest child in the crash. He empathized, and told me the sad tale of how when he returned home from the hospital, his wife was packing up to leave him, taking his only son with her. She couldn't handle his paralysis.

That was a sobering thought. At least my wife and child left this world in love with me. He had lost his family in a much more bitter way. I suddenly felt grateful and blessed for the time I had with my wife and son. I knew they were still there, watching over me and cheering me on.

My heart went out to this man from my distant past, yet I didn't know what else to say except that I was sorry. And I was. I had a more acute awareness of the suffering of others after what I had been through. Perhaps I had been wrapped up in my own misery for too long. It felt better, and far healthier, to hurt for someone else for a change. It was a huge epiphany for me that day in the gym. I had been so preoccupied with my battles that I hadn't even considered anyone else's. Perhaps the biggest gift from my ordeals was increased compassion for others.

I began to ask nurses, doctors, visitors, and other patients how they were doing, how their day was, and then really listened to their replies. I spoke to my family differently and addressed their pain and loss over all that had happened. I discovered that a big part of my pain could be swallowed up in kindness to others. By taking a genuine interest beyond what my own struggles might be and investing in someone else, my struggles actually diminished.

The days went by more quickly after that. My pain didn't go away, but I realized that everyone has some kind of hurt. Many of the people I met opened up and shared their personal challenges with me when I asked them sincere questions. I realized I had shown little concern for how my family members were doing while they had been focused on me. I had been selfish. Now, getting outside of myself turned out to be the best medicine I could possibly take for the lingering pain in my heart.

CHAPTER 13

PLANS WERE FINALLY MADE to repair my right shoulder and rotator cuff. I was worried about the surgery because I wanted so badly for things to go well. I needed the use of my right arm. My livelihood depended on it. I deserved a miracle, I felt, and made my own mind up to have one: my arm would be healed.

As the surgery approached, I welcomed the thought of the general anesthetic once again. I secretly hoped for another visit to the other side with every surgery I had, including that one. I wondered if I could get one more visit, one more hug from Tamara, and a glimpse of Griffin. My heart still longed for that place I had been so briefly.

I glanced down at my wrist where I wore the Force bracelet Spencer had made for me. I knew I was still here to be his dad. The surgery would go well and I'd come out of it with a working arm. I decided to keep my energy focused on that as well as healing completely rather than fantasizing about another peek into the hereafter. I wanted to stay in the here and now in order to get through this.

I had developed good relationships with many of the doctors. Their morning visits often turned into conversations. One of the resident doctors who had been looking after me was named Dr. Luke. He and the other physicians arrived to speak with me before the surgery. As we reviewed the procedure, he asked me to take off the Force bracelet Spencer had given me.

"You're supposed to take all your jewelry off before we go back," he reminded me.

"I know," I replied and began to untie the strings on the bracelet. "This is my *Star Wars* bracelet. My son made it for me so I would have the Force." I smiled, thinking of Spencer as I took it off and rolled the little black and white beads in my fingers. "Fix my arm, Doc," I said, laughing nervously and dropping the bracelet into his hand.

"We will. Now reach over and sign it so we cut the right one." He set the bracelet on the stand by my hospital bed. "This will be right here when you get back."

"I know. Thank you. May the Force be with you, Luke," I said. We laughed as we left the room for the procedure.

They wheeled me back and made the final preparations. I felt myself fade away as they administered the general anesthetic one more time. Everything went black as I slipped away for surgery number sixteen.

The surgery went well, but nothing but blackness surrounded me the whole time I was out. In fact, I felt like I had barely been put under when I suddenly woke again, as if only seconds had passed.

I wasn't prepared for how painful recovery from rotator cuff surgery would be. I had been through much worse, but this time around I had assumed it might be easier because I was so much stronger and healthier. However, the sting and throb of recovery from yet another surgery was all too familiar.

The rotator cuff repair would be my last surgery for a while. I'd have to wait several more months to have the colostomy taken down, and I would have reconstructive surgery on my hip and stomach at some point, but I was told that could be as much as a year away. I was beginning to sleep on my side rather than flat on my back. Even that was a welcome change. It provided much more restful nights.

My amputation site was doing well at that point, too. After several terrible bouts with infections, it was healing. Orthopedic physicians and physical therapists began the conversation with me about a prosthetic leg.

They told me I'd walk with a slight limp but would learn to master it in time. Walking was still six or more months away, but the conversation excited me. I was anxious to move forward and get to a point where I could leave the wheelchair. I thought of those who didn't have that option, and recognized how fortunate I was to eventually be able to do so.

The crazy thing at this point was what I longed for most was also one of my biggest fears: returning home. How would I function in a wheelchair in my house? How could I care for Spencer? All the logistics of actually getting back to my life were major concerns for me. We decided I would spend the remainder of the summer and into fall with Justin, and have home care nurses come to his house until I could learn to adjust to my new lifestyle.

I worked at becoming more independent than ever in the hospital. I would venture out by myself for short jaunts past the cafeteria and into the small courtyard outside the rehab wing. I loved being outside. I began to hear birds again and notice the sights and smells of nature. I was escaping from the emotional and physical pain of my own body and becoming more aware of the things around me.

I remembered how I used to be, and wondered if I would ever hike again. I had been sheltered so long in the hospital bed that the condition of my body felt new to me. I was learning how to move all over again. My mind vacillated from the immediate moments of grief to questions of what the future might be like for Spencer and me.

On one occasion, as I sat in the wheelchair feeling incredibly lonely and bleak about what life might be like at home, I noticed the rustling of the leaves in the small stand of aspen trees in the hospital courtyard. I closed my eyes and let the sound sink deeply into my ears. It was like music running through my soul.

The same breeze that moved the leaves began to rush into my hair and face. I breathed it in. As I did so I was inspired to listen, not to the leaves, but to my heart. I listened to that whisper, and as I did, I heard Tamara's voice as if it were echoing in my soul, "Each time you hear the rustling of the leaves, that's me saying, 'I love you.'"

I smiled inside, knowing my loved ones were not far away and perhaps had been there beside me the whole time. I wiped away a tear and looked at the stump of my amputated leg. I glanced at the brace holding my right leg in place. I lifted my T-shirt and observed the scars running up and down my stomach. I pulled the shirt back down and tucked it under the sling on my right arm.

I realized at that moment that I was not my broken body. I was much, much more. My spirit was intact—feeling and listening. I was becoming more enlightened than ever through the things I had experienced. I was learning so much.

Others might call me crazy for hearing messages through the breeze and the leaves of the trees, but those quiet moments spoke to my heart, saying, "no matter how bad it may seem, there is someone, somewhere who has experienced worse. No matter how intense your physical or emotional pain might be, someone is experiencing something even more intense." I breathed it in. I had become so much more aware of others through what I had suffered. My ability to empathize had been multiplied. I was learning true compassion.

I rested well that evening in my hospital bed. My room was quiet. My family was taking a well-deserved break, and no visitors came to see me. I felt far more comfortable than usual. I rolled onto my side and watched as the light through the window changed from a golden tone to a deep purple blue. I faded off to sleep.

I dreamed I was drowning. The current whisked me away uncontrollably. In desperation, I reached for anything to hold on to, a branch, a reed, or even just grass. The water rushed over me, pulling me swiftly downstream. I continued to scramble, holding my breath. I thrashed in the current in absolute panic. Suddenly, over the sound of water pouring into my ears, I thought to stop thrashing and stand up in the water.

I stopped fighting the current and let it carry me. When I relaxed and stopped struggling, I floated. I became calm. As I let my legs sink beneath me, I felt them plant on a solid riverbed. Calmly, I stood in the water to find that it was really only three or four feet deep. With my feet on firm ground, I was able to withstand the current. I felt the water rush around my waist and chest. All I had to do was stand up, and the threat disappeared.

As I stood there, my hands dragging in the flow of the river, I realized how simple my self-rescue had been. I wasn't drowning at all. The water wasn't even that deep. I stood there in my dream, having shifted from absolute panic to complete peace.

"Mr. Olsen? Mr. Olsen!" a phlebotomist said, interrupting my sleep. I woke as she nudged me. They were still doing daily blood tests. The veins in my arms were so sore, bruised, and worn out that they now were taking blood from the veins in my hands. The nurse poked at my battered arms with her gloved fingers. "What do you think? Shall we go for one in your hand again?" It all hurt. Even the little blood draws had become a hassle.

"You choose. It's all annoying at this point." I was a bit ornery, having been woken from my dream.

"I'll make it as painless as I can."

"I hope so."

"Let me show you a trick," She said kindly, and explained that poking at my veins might go easier if I went to a peaceful place in my mind. I thought of where that peaceful place would be. I considered going right back to the river in the dream I'd been having, but a different time and place came to mind immediately.

I went home, to our mountain house in Bountiful. I went to a Saturday evening several years earlier when Spencer was only four years old. He and I were sitting out on the deck, enjoying lemonade and licorice whips. I remember watching the sprinklers water the grass and listening to Tamara inside the house. She was moving about the kitchen, making banana bread. The bread smelled wonderful mixed with the scent of the freshly mowed grass.

I breathed deeply and forgot about the woman poking at the vein in my hand. My thoughts remained on the deck at home. Time stood still for me in that instant. My heart was filled with the clear certainty that being on the deck there with Spencer was as good as life could get. Tears welled up in my eyes. I could not hold back the warm feelings of joy and gratitude.

This perfect, happy place was nothing special. It was found in the simple everyday pleasure of being a husband and a dad; I continued reminiscing in my mind about being home. I could feel the heat from the warm deck on both of my feet, even the missing one, and could feel Spencer's joy and laughter rush through me as it had in that remembered evening. The experience felt like time travel, as if I was really there again.

Before I knew it, the blood had been drawn. The hospital, the surgeries, needles, and pain were all far from my mind. I had found magic in going back to the home within me.

CHAPTER 14

FAMILY MEMBERS STILL SPENT the night with me from time to time. Justin was there this time, and I always enjoyed spending time with him. We chatted for a while and discussed how I would be returning home soon. The ordeal was truly coming to an end. I was off my medications, and my body had mended in miraculous ways. As we talked, I became tired and soon faded off into a deep sleep.

It was more peaceful than most nights. I felt calm and comfortable. I was even free of most pain. I began to fall into a deep sleep, which felt so good. As I drifted off, I even thought to myself, *wow, I don't remember ever falling to sleep in such a deep, restful way.* I seemed to sink deeper and deeper into the hospital bed in pure, restful bliss.

Then I felt it: that same light that had come to me at the scene of the accident. It seemed to surround me and almost form a tunnel wherein I began to rise. *I felt this before,* I thought to myself. I seemed to rise up higher and higher. *Was this a dream?* If so, it was a very real and vivid. I found myself in that place again, full of love, light, and peace where I had said good-bye to Tamara right after the accident.

Except this time, the light began to dissolve. I could see all around me now, and there was pure beauty everywhere. I knew this place like no other. The feeling was so overwhelmingly joyful. I'd heard words like heaven, but this was even better than that: this was my home! It felt like walking through the doors of a distant childhood memory and finding Mom baking fresh bread in the kitchen with sunlight streaming through the windows and joyful music playing. I was so welcome there, so loved and embraced.

There was no more pain! I began to dance and run, feeling so joyful that I was actually home! No one came to greet me or guide me, and yet I had never felt so welcomed. I marveled at the indescribable beauty around me. It was vast and open and beautiful. I could feel, touch, and taste everything as if I had not five, but fifty senses. I was amazed.

As I walked, on two healthy, strong legs, it was a very physical experience; I could feel the energy in my muscles and the soft ground under my feet. I began to run. I enjoyed what felt like my physical body but magnified, sprinting faster and faster while not feeling winded or weary at all.

At that point, knowledge entered my consciousness that I was not there to stay. In that same instant, I noticed a long corridor to my left and I knew intuitively that I was to make my way down it. I entered into the long hallway which seemed to stretch forward almost into eternity, yet I moved down it rapidly and with ease. I saw where it came to a stop, and at the end was a rounded room. As I made my way closer, I could see that in the center was a crib. I rushed to it, peeked in, and saw something beyond joyful.

There, lying in the crib, was my son. It was little Griffin! He was alive and well. He slept as peacefully as I had seen him in the rear-view mirror just an hour before our accident. I looked at him and took in every detail: his chubby little hands, and how they lay so peacefully beside his perfect face. His mouth drew breath, raising his small back up and down. His wispy hair lay gently across the bottom of his neck. I reached into the crib and swept him up into my arms.

I could actually feel the warmth from his little body pressing against me. It was so physical, and yet beyond the physicality known in this realm; it was even more so. I could feel his breath on my neck and the smell of his delicate hair. He was so familiar and so alive! I held him close and cried tears of joy as I laid my cheek against his soft little head as we had always done in life.

I felt him breathing as he snuggled into me, his ribs rising and falling with each inhale and exhale. Not only did I feel him physically, but I also felt him spiritually. Every cell of his perfect little body was full of light and life. I felt the energy of his soul and how connected we were. I was his dad; I had taken part in creating him, and he was perfect.

The pure happiness I experienced in this moment cannot be expressed with words. Griffin had been thrown from the car in the accident. His car seat had broken apart and let him out. It was something I could never speak of. His injuries were severe, and yet here I was holding his perfect little frame. He was alive, and I was with him, holding him in this wonderful place. It was real, even super-real! I had never felt anything so intense. I sobbed with elation, holding my little boy. I closed my tear-filled eyes and breathed in how he smelled and how he felt and how everything seemed to disappear except us. I simply held him, basking in the moment. As I did, I felt a presence moving up behind us. The feelings coming from it were so powerful, so cosmic, so wise, so eternal and yet so loving and personal. It startled me.

I knew I was in the presence of God.

I did not dare turn around to look. I stood there holding my son, taking in the intense energy of that moment. I actually became fearful; I had grown up believing that God was going to judge me. Life was a test and I felt like I was failing. *I hope I'm forgiven,* I thought as I held my little boy, knowing he had left this earthly existence while I was at the driver's wheel.

I held Griffin tighter with the thought of forgiveness, and as I did, I felt light and love engulf me. "There is nothing to forgive," rang through every fiber of my soul as the being behind me moved even closer. This soul had so much light, love, and power. Still, I did not turn around. I stood there holding Griffin and feeling the overwhelming, everlasting, unconditional love, void of any judgment. It was as real as the love I felt for my own little son now in my arms.

Slowly, this magnificent, divine being stepped so close that I could feel the light emulating from its source and surrounding us. Its wisdom was overwhelming. Every cell of my body filled with truth and knowledge beyond anything I had ever felt before. As I held Griffin more tightly, this beautiful being wrapped its divine arms around and held us. I stood there holding my son and being embraced by this deity.

The magnificent soul spoke into my ear, and though it was a whisper, it was powerful. Not only did I hear it, but I felt it through my entire being. I do not have the words to write what I was told, nor could I do justice to them. I learned more in that brief encounter than I could have been taught in many lifetimes. Yet it didn't feel like learning; it was more like remembering. I knew this as it flowed through me. I saw purpose in every event of my entire life. I saw how every circumstance had been divinely provided for my learning and development.

I had the realization that I had actually taken part in creating every experience of my life. I knew I had come to this earth for only one reason, which was to learn, and everything that had ever happened to me had been a loving step in that process of my progression. Every person, every circumstance, and every incident was custom created for me, by me. It was as if the entire universe existed for my higher good and development. As this began to sink in, it felt as if Griffin merged into me and I merged into God. I felt so loved, cherished, and honored.

I realized that not only was I being embraced by Deity, but that I, myself, was divine. I knew instantly that we all are. I knew that there are no accidents in this life and everything happened for a reason. Yet I also felt the reality that I got to choose how I would experience what happened to me. Free will became the anthem of that moment, and the eternities, as if choice was the only cosmic law.

As we merged even further together, it felt as if I expanded and became all of everything that ever was. Not only was I experiencing love, I was love. Not only was I experiencing God, I was God. Not only was I at the center of the universe, I was the universe. It felt as if the entire "everything" had gathered to honor my little life, my choices, my existence, and my journey.

I couldn't help but ask the question, "Who am I that the entire universe would even care?" In that instant, the words "I *am* that I *am*," came ringing into my heart. "I am you, and you are me: we are one," vibrated into my very soul. Is this why the Master we call Jesus said, "If you've seen Me, you've seen the Father"? Did he simply realize his own divinity in the cosmic way I was now seeing the divinity of not only myself but of all humankind?

Were we all collectively and individually God, or cells in the great body of everything there is and ever would be? Are we truly empowered as divine, eternal souls to have our human experience? Could we feel every emotion, and have the gift to choose to express to the entire universe this is who I am?

As the profound questions flowed into my soul, I already knew the answers. I realized I could exercise my will in everything, even in how I felt about the wreck and the death of my family members. God didn't want me to hurt and feel put upon as if my son and wife had been taken from me. He was simply there assisting me to choose how I was going to experience it. He was providing me with the opportunity, in perfect love, to exercise my personal agency in this entire situation. Life wasn't a test: it was a gift! What I had believed so long was suddenly turned inside out in a beautiful way. Every moment of my existence was sacred, and within every moment was an opportunity to choose, to create, and to experience.

I knew my wife and son were gone. They had died months earlier, but time didn't exist where I was at that moment. Rather than having them ripped away from me, I was being given the opportunity to actually hand them over to God and let them go in peace, love, and gratitude. Everything suddenly made sense because it had divine order. I could honor our lives together, no matter how short, rather than lamenting their deaths. For there was no death; everything here was alive, always.

I felt my power as a creator and co-creator with God to literally let go of all that had happened to me. I slowly merged out of what I can only call "oneness" and began to return to the three separate entities we started as; me, holding my baby son, as God—as He—held us both.

I thought of Griffin as he had searched for Easter eggs the Sunday morning before the accident. He had toddled about, stumbling, slobbering, and calling the colored eggs "balls." *Oh, how I loved him!* He was perfect to me in every moment. I realized as I held him, and was held myself, that we are all loved in that same manner, yet magnified. We toddled about life, slobbering and stumbling while the entire universe celebrated in our simply learning to walk. We are God's toddlers and we are loved perfectly, without judgment or comparison. Each of us are in those divine arms, as Griffin was in my arms now.

Time did not matter; only love and order existed. Tamara and Griffin had come into my life as perfect teachers. In leaving me in such a way, they continued as perfect teachers to bring me to that point of remembering that I am divine and actually am the pure love I came from.

I felt the divine energy of the being behind me inviting me to let it all go and give Griffin back. Choice was honored above all else. In that perfect peace and knowledge, I hugged my little boy one last time, kissed him on the cheek, and gently laid him back into the crib. I willingly gave him up because I knew no one would ever take him away from me again. He was mine, we were one, and I was one with God.

As soon as I breathed in all that peace, I awoke back into the pain and darkness of my hospital bed, yet with a much higher perspective. I marveled at what I had just experienced. It was too real to be a dream. Griffin was alive in a place more real than anything here, and Tamara was with him. I now knew it beyond anything else.

As the years have passed, I've often wondered how I put my son back in that crib. Maybe I should have held on tighter and never let go. But in that place, it all made sense. There, I had seen my whole life. I had seen what I judged as mistakes and yet in those divine arms I knew there were no mistakes, only opportunities to learn. I decided how I felt, and that made all the difference. Even in this tragedy, I determined the outcome. I could choose to be a victim of what had happened, or create from it something far greater.

CHAPTER 15

meant what you call it? (?)

THE WEEKS FLEW BY after my epiphany, and finally I was able to return home, or at least to my brother's house where I would stay into the fall and continue healing. My brothers set up a hospital bed for me in an extra bedroom, and my stepfather, Neil, built a wheelchair ramp on the front steps. I was so eager to get home, yet scared to leave the hospital. I had spent over five months there; it had almost become home.

My brothers loaded up all my things, wheeled me down the long hallways of the hospital, and lifted me into the car. They literally had to lift me. With my left leg amputated, my right arm immobilized, and my right leg still in a brace, there was no way I could transfer myself from the wheelchair into the car.

We began the drive to my brother's house, which was about forty minutes from the hospital. I nearly got carsick from the simple motion of the ride, and I had to steady myself on the seat with my left arm. Riding with only one leg was different. I looked down at the empty place where my leg had been and at the vacant spot on the car floor mat where my foot would have gone. Things were going to be different now, but I was thankful to be moving forward.

I watched out the window at all the cars and people moving about, living their day-to-day lives. Did they realize how quickly things could change? In a moment, everything could be different. What were their challenges, their joys, their dreams and fears? Where all those people any different from me, really?

I knew we were all connected, so was there any difference anyway? Did my triumphs raise them is some way? Did theirs raise me? Did we literally feed each others' fears based on our judgments? Did we raise each other up based on how we lived our lives? I watched the sun flashing in and out of the windows as we passed trees and other cars. Everything seemed to be in slow motion.

As we came closer to my brother's house, I began to worry about how Spencer might feel, given how I'd changed. Would he really accept me as I was? I'd be using an electric wheelchair and have one leg and an unusable right arm. I looked a bit like a monster with all the scars, bandages, and my missing limb. I would no longer be the dad who played catch with him and roughhoused on the lawn. I couldn't throw him high into the air to catch him safely in my arms. I would no longer be the dad who could sling him over my shoulder and carry him up the stairs to tuck him into bed at night.

How would it be? Could he accept me the way I was now, and how might he feel out in public? Would he be embarrassed to be with me at the grocery store or at school programs? Would I be a dad he could be proud of, or would he shy away and become detached? It was one thing for him to visit me in the hospital, but now I was on his turf in the real world.

As we pulled up into the driveway, my brothers got out to collect the wheelchair. I saw Spencer watching from the front window of the house. I was anxious to see him but so nervous about how he might accept me. My brothers literally lifted me from the car seat into the wheelchair. I saw Spencer still looking out the window as all this was taking place. I noticed as he watched his uncles, my brothers, have to lift me, being powerless on my own.

As they set me in the wheelchair, I worked to get adjusted into the seat and unlocked the wheels for the ride up the ramp. As I did so, the front door swung open and Spencer came running out. He ran down the walk toward me. I anticipated him jumping onto my lap, but instead, he flew right past me. My fears were realized: *being like this is too much for him,* I thought. *No way can he accept me the way I am now in the real world. It doesn't work for him.* My heart sank.

I watched as he ran past me, continuing to the other side of the street.

I supposed he was running away from it all, trying to remove himself from the painful situation of seeing his dad helplessly lifted from the car and into the wheelchair. I began to make my way to the ramp with the electric wheelchair to get out of sight as quickly as possible. As I made the turn to go up the ramp, I looked across the road one more time to locate Spencer. Much to my surprise, he was running from house to house, banging on all the neighborhood doors and yelling at the top of his lungs.

"Come out!" he shouted for everyone to hear. "My dad is home! My dad is home! Come out and see my dad!"

He went from neighbor to neighbor, darting back and forth. "Come see my dad!" His voice rang happily down the street, echoing off the asphalt. "Come see my dad! He's the toughest man in the world!"

Finally, after making the rounds, he ran back to me and threw himself onto my lap. I still had the staples up my belly from the abdominal surgery. The pain about killed me when he launched his tiny body against my chest and threw his arms around my neck, but the embrace was such a welcome reception. I laughed and looked at him.

"Are you okay, Son?" I asked. "Are you going to be okay with your dad like this?"

We still laugh at his reply to this day: he smiled and said, "Dad, if you were nothing but a big puddle of blood, I would still love you."

I hugged him tightly and laughed aloud. My laughter turned to grateful tears as I held my surviving boy on my lap and hugged him close to me exactly as I had held Griffin in my amazing dream. I had a huge epiphany in that moment: I realized that holding my surviving son from my wheelchair in this realm was no less divine than holding my deceased son in those heavenly realms.

In fact, heaven was right here; there was nowhere to go, nothing to become. It was divine to simply be in that moment and experience the miracle of being alive feeling unconditional love right here, right now.

I loved Spencer so much. He was such a source of strength for me. I knew I had survived for him as well as for myself. It was for no grander reason than to simply be his dad. And what grander reason is there?

THE SUMMER MOVED ON. Nurses and physical therapists came to the house every day to attend to my still-healing wounds and to assist me with physical therapy. Others still had to bathe me, sometimes dress me, and work on my mending body. My arm was healing well, though; I was moving it and making progress toward using it. I got stronger on my one remaining leg, too. I still made regular hospital visits, but I was healing both physically and emotionally. I desired to return home to my own house and get Spencer back into his regular school. I was driven to become independent and stop having to be cared for and waited upon.

Home was always on my mind. As soon as we were able, I wanted to drive to my home and begin preparations to move back in. That first trip was devastating, however. As I entered the house, Griffin's toys were still on the front room floor. Neighbors and family had cared for things over those long months, but out of respect for our family, they left everything as it was the day we had left the house for St. George. It didn't seem right for anyone except me to put anything away. As hard as it was to see those things, I was glad they'd left them. I could hear Griffin's laughter as I looked at the toys. The memories were happy ones, but the pain was still so real. Even with what I had experienced, I still had so much grief and regret, and so much healing to do.

Our home was three stories, and the bedrooms were on the upper floors. My brothers lifted me up the stairs to the master bedroom. Tamara had laid one of her sweaters over a chair by the bed to dry the day before we left. My heart winced at seeing that; she wouldn't be wearing it ever again. I thought of her delicate hands and how she placed it with such care. Like the laughter in Griffin's toys, the sweater represented the order, beauty, and joy Tamara had brought to my life. I actually left the toys and the sweater as they were for quite some time. I felt closer to my wife and son, somehow, by leaving the things they had last touched right where they had set them.

I had good neighbors who had surprised me with a wheelchair ramp at my home, too, so I could easily get into my house. Many people had done so much to see to my comfort and healing. I felt their love, and a deeper appreciation for the little things in life, especially the acts of kindness that had been performed on my behalf. It gave me a greater desire to serve others and make a difference in the lives of people who may be hurting like I had been and still was.

Spencer and I slowly made the transition home, sometimes only staying the weekend and going back to my brother's during the week, but eventually we moved back home permanently. It felt good to be home. I would spend hours on the back deck, looking over the view and watching the sunsets. The hardest time was at night. The queen bed felt big and empty to me. Loneliness would often sink in during those hours, so I often slept in the recliner in the front room on the main level of the house rather than up the stairs in my bedroom.

Eventually, I was well enough to return to work. I was still in a wheelchair and had limited use of my right arm, but it was good to be back. My friends at work took turns driving me to and from the office. My arm wasn't well enough for me to drive a car, but I was becoming productive at work, which helped the days go by more easily.

Spencer was back at school with old friends and seemed to be doing well. I started driving again in a matter of months, which gave me new freedom. I was finally strong enough to transfer myself from the wheelchair to the car, and since the car was an automatic transmission, I could drive quite well with only my right foot.

Once inside the house, I spent most of my time on the main level, but had developed an awkward way of scooting up the stairs on my rear end when I wanted to go up to the bedroom.

A neighboring family, and good friends of ours, cared for Spencer after school until I could get home from work. The amount of kindness I was shown during that time, still astounds me. People were so willing to offer assistance.

One night, the family that was looking after Spencer made an extra pan of enchiladas and sent them home with us for dinner. I sent Spencer in ahead of me through the garage with the pan of enchiladas to unlock the door while I parked the car and transferred into the wheelchair.

As he turned with the hot pan of enchiladas to hold the door for me, the padded mitt slipped, exposing his hand to the hot pan. He yelled out and dropped the pan.

Helplessly, I watched as he shook his burned hand and the cheesy, red enchilada sauce splattered on the carpet. I hopped out of the chair and scooted on my rear end to Spencer to see that his hand was okay. It was fine, but Spencer was devastated. His countenance had fallen into complete shame. I saw tears begin to well up in his eyes as he watched our colorful Mexican dinner oozing into our off-white carpet.

He ran and got dish towels, and we started the cleanup process. I mopped it up the best I could, scooting around on the floor while Spencer went back and forth to the kitchen sink, rinsing out the towels.

By the time we finished, it was past Spencer's bedtime, so I sent him to bed and watched as he walked up the two flights of stairs to his own room. As he made his way up, his seven-year-old head hung in shame for having dropped the dinner pan. He looked so small and lonely. The sadness of all that had happened began to overtake me again.

Is this too much for him? I thought. *Is it too much for me?* Why did he have to grow up so fast? How would he ever know how wonderful his mother was, or how brilliant his little brother might have been? And was it fair for him to be caring for me like this at such a young age?

I was again overcome with sadness and regret. I crawled out of the wheelchair and lay on the ground, breaking inside. I couldn't even get up the stairs to tuck him into bed properly. I wanted to see that he was at least okay up in his room all by himself. I composed myself long enough to shout good night up to him. He shouted back, "Love you too, Dad, and sorry about dropping the enchiladas."

I assured him that it was fine, nothing at all to worry about, but then the depths of all that had happened swept over me. As soon as I knew he was sleeping, I drifted into a convulsing, crying fit that seemed to literally shake the earth. How was I ever going to raise him on my own? Would he eventually forget his mother? Would he ever remember her softness or her love? Would he remember their walks, or making banana bread together, or the way he used to kiss her cheek and laugh when they danced together? Would I forget these things? The pain of it was too much.

I poured my heart out to God, not asking for anything or even expecting anything, simply gushing out my soul to the only listening ear that could possibly understand. As I finally shed all the tears I had left and became quiet, a strange thing happened. I don't often hear voices, but I heard this one, and it consisted of the same energy as the voice that whispered in my ears when I held Griffin in that other realm. It was not a harsh voice, but the loving voice of a father who knew me perfectly. He only said two words, but they were as loud and clear as I have heard anything.

He simply said, "Choose joy."

It was a simple request, and yet again, all about my choice. Joy was there if I only decided to see it and grasp it. The universe gave me that option. I didn't know all of life's challenges, but I always got to determine how I would deal with them.

CHAPTER 16

After several months, doctors were able to repair my intestines and take down my colostomy. Reconstructive surgery was done on my stomach and hip as well. Months of physical therapy restored almost 70 percent usage of my right arm.

I was learning how to walk all over again using a prosthetic limb. The first people I wanted to show were my brothers. I had been practicing at the physical therapist's between parallel bars to hold myself up, but I felt I was ready for a solo voyage.

Justin came to my house. I sat on the edge of the bed as I put on the prosthesis, explaining how it worked. I stood up, and Justin smiled the most amazing grin.

"I forgot you were actually that tall!" he laughed.

I took one step, then another, then two more. I became a bit cocky and walked across the room, only to trip and fall flat on my face. It hurt, but in total tough-guy fashion, I struggled back onto my hands and knees as quickly as I could. I managed to get back up on my one good knee before Justin reached me. He pulled me the rest of the way up and we hugged each other, laughing joyfully.

"That hurt! I fell pretty hard," I said through our laughter.

"Yes, you did, big brother," Justin agreed. "But you got back up."

The following months were long and difficult even with all I had experienced. Getting used to my body and how it worked now was a long progress. I spent months with physical therapists and occupational therapists learning how to walk. I continued using my right arm. Balance was also new as I tried to master steadying myself on one leg when not using the prosthetic limb. Simple things like taking a shower were now an event. Standing on soapy, wet tile with one foot, balancing while washing was a whole new game. Of course, we installed grip bars and even put a stool in the shower for me to sit on if it became too difficult.

Everything was a new chain of challenges for me to face. Combing my hair and shaving with only my left hand without the full use of my right arm was a challenge, as was carrying even light objects while maintaining balance on the prosthetic limb. Dealing with phantom pain in the amputated leg while still working to strengthen my badly injured right leg was a test, too. Physical pain was a part of every waking hour.

Beyond the physical challenges were the emotional rollercoasters. The grief was still hitting in huge waves that were overwhelming for me. A random song would come on the radio, or I would see something while out and about; a toddler playing with his mother, people jogging along the boulevard, the tree Tamara and I planted together. I was surrounded by reminders. I can't even count how many nights I cried myself to sleep. I continually had thoughts of escaping it all and going back to those realms of peace. I was suicidal often, but Spencer kept me here. Watching him grow was still a joy and my strongest anchor to this realm.

I had good friends and family to support me as well. Even my doctors had become my friends. My original ER doctor would stop by for visits, which often turned into long discussions. We wouldn't talk about the accident in detail, nor the events surrounding it; our conversations were far more spiritual in nature. I knew he had experienced Tamara's soul in the ER, and that was enough for me to trust him. I felt he somehow knew my soul as well.

We'd talk about how to stay connected to heaven from this realm, as well as how to deal with the emotional pain and finding purpose in the wake of loss. He inspired me to recognize what I was learning and how my soul was growing. I found it interesting that my ER doctor would end up being the one I felt safe sharing everything with. Perhaps it was his openness to what I had experienced and his lack of judgment about what I had to share that made it easy. Plus, he wasn't family.

As I shared very personal things with my closest family members, of course, they lovingly listened and agreed; that's how my family is. My brothers were my closest friends, and my mom and dad were supportive no matter what. Yet there was power in sharing these spiritual and emotional aspects of my current challenges with what was basically a stranger. My doctor had no history with me beyond what he had encountered in the trauma room the day of the accident. He was a completely unbiased audience. The fact that we both grew up in small, rural towns in Utah and had similar interests, seemed like a coincidence at that point.

Sharing my deepest experiences and my personal feelings surrounding those experiences with a credible medical professional without being judged or laughed at felt liberating. It was the kindness of the universe manifested once again in the simple synchronicity of life. This man also had similar life experiences to my own, and could relate to what I was sharing in a unique, personal way.

I realized that everything I knew had been turned upside down, and I would never have the same life as before. There were so few people I could discuss that with. And then there was the nature of my profound experiences on the other side. How does one relate to that? Religion didn't necessarily make sense anymore. The truth and knowledge that had surrounded me and literally become a part of me while in the other realms with Griffin was not common lunch conversations in most circles. Nor could I necessarily articulate these revelations in a way that even made sense to me, let alone others. It's like I'd seen the sum, but was still gathering all the formulaic parts of the equation.

I studied many things, looking for answers even though I already knew the end result. I had experienced the unconditional love of God and the entire universe, but little of it matched with life now and what I was experiencing here in this realm. Where was all the unconditional love and majesty? Where was all the connection? I felt like a stranger in a strange land. I knew what I knew with all my heart, but I could not articulate it, nor did I know who I could trust to even discuss it with. I kept things to myself, only mentioning minor, vague details with my closest friends and family members. And even then, I held back, never going too deep into all the questions I had already experienced the answers to.

I learned to speak in a language others could better comprehend even though I would usually only share bits and pieces of the entire story (if I spoke about any of it at all). I found it was much easier to just not get into it and embrace the mundane tasks of day-to-day life and conversations. Keeping things trivial was the easiest route.

Who were my top picks for the Final Four Brackets? What was my take on the *Monday Night Football* game? Or what were the best films out in the cinema at the moment? I wanted normal and calm, but my mind never stopped grappling with how to make sense of everything that had happened to me. On the outside, everyone spoke of how well I was doing, of how miraculously I had healed. They had no idea that there were still splinters that pierced my heart and soul.

I learned to love seclusion. Nature was my refuge. Thank goodness I lived in the mountains where peace and quiet were in my backyard. I learned to see sunsets as magnificent paintings in the sky. Every rainstorm was a miracle. The way the wildflowers grew, the leaves on the trees danced, and the birds mingled in the landscape were all big parts of my healing. I was simply finding escape from my mind and my ego to connect with that part of me that had always existed and was here only visiting from those higher realms.

I eventually eased my way back into full-time work and driving my own car. Spencer was still the biggest thing in my life, though I had to hire a good nanny for him. Things settled down for us. Our evenings at home returned to playful times together. Our favorite thing to do was to play laser tag with the new *Star Wars* gun set he'd gotten for Christmas. I'd stay somewhat stationary behind the couch or a chair while Spencer ran all around the house attempting to shoot me without me tagging him with a laser beam first. At least he found joy in playing with new toys again, and I always loved his company.

However, that first Christmas back home was the roughest few weeks for me. There were plenty of visitors, and I had time off to spend with Spencer, but words cannot describe how truly lonely I felt. After I'd spend time with my son and he went to bed, my thoughts would turn again to the stars, how vast the universe was, and how alone I seemed to be in it. The emptiness was the worst part. Even though I had healed really well physically, I was still so torn open emotionally.

Each day was long and the nights were longer. The days became weeks, then months, and eventually I realized I was still counting them: days since the accident, weeks, months, then six months, even seven, eight, and nine. Christmas was the nine-month mark. I was walking again, though I often used a cane. I was back at work in full capacity, which I must mention had been a long road. I knew my business partners had about given up on me many times.

I struggled to keep my head clear and concentrate on what was expected of me. Some days simply getting to the office was about all my emotions could handle. I'd close the door, turn the music on, and cry, or just sit, not contributing much at all. All I could do was simply breathe. I suppose it's a blessing I was an owner or I may well have been fired. Even with all I had experienced spiritually, life was still challenging. In fact, in some ways it was even more so. My business partners had been kind and patient, and I was grateful for that.

It felt as if I was constantly homesick for Tamara and Griffin, not to mention realms of light where I had felt so much and known so much light. Where was all that here, in this realm? I was also very physically lonely. Where were those arms that held me, the lips that kissed me, the laughter and deep conversation? What good was knowing all the love I had experienced in those realms without someone here to share it with? The best way to describe the year following the accident was solitude. I was surrounded by family, friends, and good neighbors, yet I felt completely alone. Even Spencer could never fill the void that was gaping invisibly within me.

I'd often sit alone on our back deck at night, looking at the star-filled sky, wondering how to make sense of everything I was feeling. I still worried a lot about Spencer, too. He seemed to be doing well, but I knew he struggled much the same as I did. We were going through the motions of having healed and making a life, but I knew we weren't; we were only pretending. It felt so much like shear panic inside while keeping a strong face on the outside. In so many ways it was like living a lie.

"We are doing really well," I would reply when anyone inquired. "Things are going great." All the while I felt moments away from literally falling apart at the seams. When would it ever go away? Nearly a year had passed. I knew I'd never get over it, but I wanted to at least get used to it.

I looked for Tamara and Griffin in everything, but they were gone. It felt so permanent. I simply had to keep breathing until I could somehow drift off to sleep, but then morning would always come. Daylight would bring the darkness of my reality, and I never truly woke from the bad dream. A full year passed since the day of the accident. It didn't feel at all like a benchmark, only another inhale and exhale in a sea of one breath to the next.

CHAPTER 17

S UNLIGHT CREPT INTO MY dark room. I'd already been semi-awake for some time, simply not willing to get up. I took a deep breath and felt my chest rise and expand effortlessly. Taking air in felt good. With the pulmonary embolisms, life-threatening bouts with pneumonia, and the injuries my ribs and chest had sustained, breathing without pain or coughing was liberating.

I exhaled and opened my eyes, focusing out the open bedroom window on the wild grasses that had begun to sprout up on the back hill. I took another deep breath and came into full consciousness. Mornings were a reminder that what had happened was my life now. I believed I would eventually wake up from the nightmare; however, the light coming in from the small, east-facing window made it clear that the nightmare was my reality.

I took another deep breath and looked at the long shadows created by the light coming into the room. Today felt different, welcoming. I felt alive—which I hadn't felt since the accident. I leaned up on my left arm to take another look at the back hill. I felt distanced from all the pain, as if today I was only observing my life rather than living it.

It was a refreshing reprieve from the normal routine of opening my eyes, yet again, to the emptiness of what had happened. It had been almost a year since the accident. I had experienced so much grief and regret over those long months that I believed it would never end. Yet today the air smelled of

Russian olive trees was filled with the still energy of spring and the electric anticipation of rebirth. I heard birds singing.

I sat up and swung my leg out of bed. I felt the coolness of the floor as I stood up, bracing myself on the nightstand to reach for my crutches. I felt as if I were taking my first steps. I paused, steadying myself for a moment, and looked about the room. I saw reminders of Griffin and Tamara. Griffin's small handprints were still on the full-length mirror in the closet, and Tamara's sweater was still neatly laid over the chair next to the bed, just as she left it the day before the accident. I had grieved for so long, yet today I felt their presence stronger than ever.

I felt my lungs expand with life again as I breathed in the spring air, placed my crutches under my arms, and hobbled on my one leg toward the shower. The water felt invigorating on my chest and the back of my neck. I felt gratitude as I dried off, put on my prosthetic leg, and dressed for the day. Driving into the city felt brighter. I turned on music. Even walking with my cane into the office that morning was easier. My desk seemed to greet me; the energy of having work to do felt good.

I popped into coworkers' offices to say hello. They invited me to join them for lunch at a fancy restaurant we'd been invited to. I declined, but as they insisted, spring and their warm beckoning became so welcoming I could not refuse. What was it about this day that felt so different? The pain and grief now seemed numbed by the energy that had surrounded me from the time I opened my eyes. The hours rolled along easily.

We drove to the New Yorker restaurant and were greeted by the hostess, who told us we could sit in the private dining room wherever we liked. Being the shy one, I took a seat at the back corner of the room to watch the whole ritual. When a woman entered the room carrying presentation books, my attention was diverted from the others to her. She paused to set the books down on the table near me. I was mesmerized as she continued to make her way around the room. I actually felt her energy. She captivated me. She had stunning, clear-blue eyes and blonde, shoulder-length hair. The details of her face were striking and well-defined.

She was thin but shapely and had moved about the room with the grace of an angel. She carried a presence that both uncontrollably drew me in and intimidated me at the same time. She looked over at me. I wanted to speak to her but didn't know what to say. "Hello," would have been obvious, but I sat in silence, watching her.

The strangest feeling of déjà vu overcame me. It was like I was remembering her even though I didn't know her name. *Was I crazy?*

The room filled up, and the luncheon began. By the time everyone had taken their seats, only one seat was left across from me. The attractive woman was still on her feet, ready to take charge. She welcomed everyone, passed out the presentation books, and then made her way to the only remaining empty seat, right across the table from me. I couldn't stop looking at her eyes. They were piercing but so beautiful.

It had been a year since the accident. Was I allowed to look at a woman like this? Here I sat across from a stranger, still engulfed in my new feelings of the day. I watched as she cut her steak into small, bite-sized pieces. She was delicate but deliberate. I first noticed her hands. They were feminine but no stranger to hard work. Her nails weren't false or fancy but well-kept. I looked at her trim, fit arms as she sawed at the steak, cutting several small pieces at a time before she'd dip one into the silver relish dish of ketchup on her plate. Ketchup, on a USDA Prime Choice New York strip? I found it strange and amusing, yet somehow endearing.

"Hi, my name is Jeff," I said politely and reached across the table to shake her hand. She put down her fork and took my hand with a firm but feminine handshake.

"I'm Tonya," she replied. "Pleased to meet you." Her voice was polite yet so inviting. It sounded like a sweet song with just a hint of raspiness. Why was I feeling her voice like that, as if a familiar song had come on the radio reminding me of a joyful memory?

We returned to our meals and sat in awkward silence for a few brief seconds before I remembered her mentioning she was not from here in the short presentation she gave before sitting down.

"So how long have you been in Utah?" I asked her as I swallowed and wiped the corner of my mouth with the white linen napkin.

"Not long," she replied. "And yet long enough. I'm not sure I like it here. In fact, I'm leaving soon to live with my sister in Arizona. I'll be making the official announcement today at this luncheon. I intend to move as soon as next month."

"Wow. At least you'll be moving to warmer weather," I remarked.

"Yes, and new possibilities. I came out here for work—and for a guy—but things haven't worked out. And Utah's strange. It's been difficult meeting people here. You either have to be in a bar or at church, and I'm not necessarily comfortable in either place."

She dipped another small piece of steak in ketchup and bit it off the fork with her teeth so as to not smear her lipstick. She lifted her hand to cover her mouth while she chewed and asked, "What do you do?"

"Oh, lots of things, I guess. By day, I'm a creative director at a local ad agency. At night, however, I transform into a single dad." I paused. The words were still painful to say, even after a year. Verbalizing it brought the pain of what had happened back to the surface. "I was widowed a year ago. I'm still working to find 'normal' I guess."

She stopped chewing, swallowed hard, and looked at me. "I'm sorry," she said.

I shook my head. "It's not your fault."

I always felt the sting of my own remorse whenever someone apologized. I was driving the car when my wife and toddler son were killed in the accident. No one felt as sorry as I did.

I watched again as she cut more small pieces from the steak. I noticed in slow motion all the details of her hands, arms, and face as that powerful déjà vu hit again. I looked at her eyes. Memories of the first time I met Tamara came rushing over me.

That was the last time I had overwhelming feelings like this. The same striking jolt that was rushing through me now had happened nearly thirteen years earlier when I felt the rush of seeing her sky-blue eyes as Tamara pulled her blonde bangs back to look at me. I recalled her smile, her soft confidence, and that feeling of floating yet being more solidly planted on the ground than ever before.

I remembered the way she smelled and how my soul seemed to jump when I simply caught her glance. I recalled the feeling of those warm goosebumps down the small of my back and that sense of knowing a secret, but I wasn't sure what it was. And now it was rushing over me again. I immersed myself in the familiar recollection, but why was I feeling such things? Was it the conversation and admitting I was widowed? I wasn't sure, but I felt that same intense tingle of "knowing" all over again.

I glanced back up at the woman sitting across from me, who was scooping vegetables onto her fork. Perhaps she looked like Tamara, at least a little bit. Maybe that's what took me by surprise. I sat silently, staring at her. She had the same stunning blue eyes, but she projected a new feeling altogether. She was foreign yet familiar, and kind, yet driven. She had the same physical build as Tamara but was unique in every way.

Everything around her seemed to darken, as if she sat under a spotlight. What was going on? Why was this happening? I had sat with and spoken to other women over those long, lonely months. So why did I have all these feelings now, and why was it so similar to the first time I met my late wife?

I'm losing it, I thought to myself. *I really must be going crazy. This woman—a stranger—sits across from me, and I can't even concentrate on the conversation because of all the emotions flooding over me.*

I quickly changed the subject. "How's the steak?" I asked.

"Good, actually. The best I've had in a long time," she replied.

She looked up at me. I noticed her stunning blue eyes again, and felt another deep ping in my core. She stabbed another small piece of steak with her fork, swirled it into the dish of ketchup, and popped it into her mouth, this time paying no mind to her lipstick. She also gracefully swept her bangs aside to look at me.

"How long have you been in advertising?" she continued as she chewed on the steak. I could tell she wanted to escape the widower topic and find much more comfortable ground to tread on, avoiding the real questions she wanted to ask. How many children did I have? How was I widowed? What happened? I'm sure she also felt my anxiety about the topic and purposely kept things at shallow small talk for my sake.

"Over ten years now," I answered. "I started right out of college, and it's all I've ever done."

I did my best to push away the overwhelming yet familiar feelings and finished my food. At this point, I simply wanted to escape these strange emotions and get back to the office. It was too much to take in. I wiped my mouth again with the napkin and pushed back my chair. "It was a pleasure meeting you," I said, gripping my cane to find my balance as I stood up on my prosthetic leg. "Thank you for sitting by me." I reached out to shake her hand. "Here's to Salt Lake City treating you better the rest of your stay."

"Yes, thank you," she said as she reached down beside her chair into her bag to pull out a business card. She handed me the card and smiled. "Call me if you need any specifications on designer paper or samples of any kind."

"Will do," I replied as I took the card and smiled back at her.

I turned and walked away, wondering whether she noticed my limp as I did so. I was doing my best to let go of the overwhelming feelings I'd been having. Why do I care? I felt awkward, and the whole ordeal had put me in a bit of a funk.

I began locating my work associates as they mingled and said their good-byes. I looked back one more time at the woman I'd just met and felt that same bolt of recognition that was so hauntingly familiar. I shook my head and continued limping to the reception area to wait for the others.

I looked at the business card she'd handed me. "Tonya Skubic," I said under my breath, rubbing my thumb over the raised letters on the thick paper. I put the card in my pocket and decided to make my way to the parking garage. I was still learning to walk on the artificial limb and wanted to take my time so I wouldn't fall or lose my balance. I stumbled often and didn't want to cause a scene in front of the lunch crowd.

I easily made it to my truck and began driving back toward the office.

I probably should have stayed behind and not gone to lunch, I thought as I made the turn into our office parking lot, still wondering why I had felt so strongly toward Tonya and why she was lingering in my mind. *I definitely do not get out enough*, I figured as I parked and made my way back to my desk.

CHAPTER 18

IT WAS ALMOST TWO when I sat down and looked at my computer screen. I had plenty to do and didn't want the extended lunch break to put me further behind in getting home to my eight-year-old. The workday took over, and soon it was after six. I knew Spencer would be waiting at home, so I put the day's unfinished layouts aside and headed to the parking lot to get into my truck. Spring was still in the air and was as powerful as it had been that morning. The sun had started to set, but it was still warm enough that I felt the heat of its low rays on my shoulders as I crossed the street to the parking lot.

I enjoyed driving again. I purchased a truck after the accident because I found that stepping up into a truck with my one leg was much easier than bending down to sit in a lower-profile car. I'd been driving for a few months now, and it was liberating to be out of a wheelchair, to learn to walk, and to be independent enough to not rely on family and friends for transportation. I had worried about getting behind the wheel again; the memory of the accident was still painful. But it was an important step in my recovery, and at this point driving became natural again. The fear of the crash subsided.

I reached up to switch on the radio, but I still could not lift my right arm high enough to press the knob. My arm had been nearly torn off in the accident. I let go of the wheel briefly to use my left arm to assist my right arm to the height of the radio switch on the dash. I was even okay with letting go of the wheel for a brief second.

As I drove home, I reflected on the day and the woman I had met, but my thoughts quickly refocused on Spencer as soon as I parked and came into the house. When I came through the door to greet him, he was enjoying a large bowl of macaroni and cheese that the nanny had made. We reviewed the day's homework, then we both sat in the big recliner in the front room to watch television for a while before bed.

I was thankful that Spencer seemed to be doing so well, but there was still a sadness and emptiness in our home since it had become just the two of us. We developed a routine, which covered the dull sting of it all. We sat together a lot and did things to keep us occupied every night until it was time to sleep. Then I would put him to bed and enter into the thick silence of the house, dealing with my own lingering emotions.

With everything quiet, I made my way up the stairs to my bedroom. It still took a bit to navigate the stairs with my artificial leg, but I was getting better. I concentrated on taking one step at a time and making sure I had the false leg securely under me before I took the next step up. I'd never really noticed the sturdy handrails before the accident, but I was glad they were there now to assist me.

As I sat on the bed and took off my prosthesis, I wondered if I would ever feel whole again. I had so many powerful, spiritual experiences over the long months of my physical recovery, but I still had far to go. As I undressed, I looked at the stump that once was my leg and all the scars on my body. A lot of things had changed for me, but I was adapting to my new life.

I reflected again on the woman I'd met at lunch that day: *Tonya*. Why did she linger in my mind? I looked at the sweater Tamara had left on the chair next to the bed. Would I ever have the courage to put it away? I reached down to the side of the bed where my clothes lay. I took out the business card and looked at her name again, then set it on my nightstand. Why had I experienced such strong feelings while sitting across from Tonya? Was I feeling too lonely? Was I even emotionally healthy? Maybe I was actually losing my mind while I put up a strong front of a courageous recovery.

I turned off the lamp and lay uneasily in the darkness. I looked out the big bedroom window. My glance wandered upward to the stars I could see just over the hill behind our house. Were they still watching me? Were Tamara and Griffin aware of my days and long, restless nights? I knew they were there, based on my experiences, but did they look over me now?

The magic of that morning had vanished into the dark night. I rolled on my side in bed and reached down to rub the sore end of my amputated leg. The phantom pains were sometimes unbearable—strange, electric-shock sensations of pain. Sometimes I experienced even stranger sensations as specific as an itch on my third toe, a charley horse in my calf, or even a pebble in my shoe, yet the leg wasn't even there. I wondered why the pain was so intense, specific, and real. Perhaps it was my spirit simply screaming for the missing limb? Or maybe it was the dull pain of my soul crying out for the love it once knew but had lost?

I rolled onto my back again and took one last look at the stars out the window. I said a silent prayer for Spencer for his emotional healing as I gazed into the heavens. I hoped he was doing better than I was. We didn't really talk about the accident. He avoided it even when I got the courage to bring it up. It was just too painful for either of us, so we did our best to look forward and not live in the tragedy of the past.

My last conscious thoughts wandered to the luncheon. The name on the card and the feel of those raised letters played over in my mind. *Tonya*. I gazed at the card, sitting in the partial darkness on the nightstand. I could still see it from the moonlight coming through the window. I finally faded into rest, never sure if I was really sleeping or only quieting my mind for a while from the endless questions and emotional wounds that still existed in spite of all I knew.

CHAPTER 19

THE EARLY MORNING LIGHT came in through the window. I sat up quickly to check the time and hollered up the half flight of stairs for Spencer to get up for school. He was always responsive, and I could hear him immediately jump out of bed to run into his bathroom, shower, and get ready. I was lucky; he was easy to get going and always took the initiative to get himself out the door. He'd been helpful like that since we'd returned home. He knew my physical condition was far from what it used to be and wanted to assist me in every way.

After the shower, I dressed as quickly as I could but was frustrated at the time it took. Putting my prosthetic leg on properly was not something I could do quickly. Even after I got the prosthetic leg on, I still could not lift my right arm above my head due to the injuries I sustained in my shoulder. I finally got myself put together and quickly reached for my cane when I noticed Tonya's business card still sitting on my nightstand.

I had the overwhelming feeling I should call her. I paused for a moment, then grabbed the card and stuffed it in my pocket as I headed to the main level of the house to meet my son. The time it took me to get ready had put us behind, so we grabbed a simple breakfast of Pop Tarts as we headed out the door and drove to Spencer's school.

I pulled up to the school, dropped Spencer off, and watched as he walked slowly to the playground where many of the kids would play before the bell rang. Spencer was not a popular child, and many of his peers teased him. The fact that his dad was now crippled and his mother and brother had been killed didn't help matters. It gave the other kids more fodder to ostracize him and treat him differently. They could be so unkind. Part of me wanted to get out and reprimand the kids as they teased or pushed at him, but I knew in my heart that if I did, it would only make things worse.

Spencer became agitated when I spoke of the accident to anyone outside of our immediate family. He didn't want anyone to know about the crash or our loss, even though the entire community was aware of it by now. Somehow, he wanted life to just move on as if nothing had happened. Anytime I'd speak of it in front of him, he'd pull my sleeve and give me that look that clearly said, "Dad, don't."

It made me feel so helpless. Was he actually handling it better than I was, or did he feel my shame and guilt which still lingered because I was driving the car? I felt like he wanted to forget, and yet I wanted to see that we always remembered. Was I making it worse for him? Was my pain keeping his wounds infected?

When I asked him why and explained that it was healthy to talk about things, Spencer simply disagreed and said he didn't want people to know. I think it made him feel even more awkward and different than he felt already. The last thing I wanted to do was make things worse for him, so I too pushed the past away in an effort to hide my own pain.

When I arrived at work, the morning was much like any other day. The joy of spring and the vibrant energy of the day before had come and gone like a gentle breeze; emptiness and guilt had found their way back. I crossed the street and went up to the big freight elevator at the back of the building. I avoided climbing the three flights of stairs I once raced up to get to our offices on the third floor.

Many people had already arrived, and I went straight to my office to start on my emails and look at the day's schedule. I reached into my pocket to take out my keys and felt the business card again. I took it out with the keys and set them both on my desk. *Why was I so compelled to call her?* The number glared at me as I sat down. I attempted to ignore it.

I reached for my keyboard and noticed my wedding band still on my left hand. Why call anyway? She'd already told me she was leaving soon to take a different job. Maybe that's why it felt safe. What harm would there be in simply reaching out? I could be a short-term friend with no motives during the few weeks she had left in town.

I began scrolling through my email. I could use some company without any attachments or expectations. I wished the voice in my head would be quiet. I stopped typing, shifted in my chair, and looked down at my shoes. The conversation in my mind did not quiet, but instead shifted. I just sat there, looking at my shoes and wondering if others could tell which one was my fake foot with my shoes on.

"Hey, we're in the War Room in three minutes!" Mike, one of my work colleagues, shouted into my office from the hallway, snapping me back to reality.

"Got it," I said. "Be right there."

I made my way to the room the others were in. I sat in the meeting feeling relief from the nagging voice in my head. Somehow keeping busy calmed me, but total focus was difficult. Most days held that strange feeling of walking into a room to get something and suddenly forgetting what you were looking for. Today became the same, except I knew what I was looking for. The room just didn't exist where I would find it.

The day began to sweep me away, and I lost myself in the chaos. My business partners were kind and understanding. They couldn't possibly grasp all I was dealing with, but they were patient, knowing that even at my best, I was not "all there" at times.

I did what I could to contribute in meaningful ways, but there were still days that I had to close my door and be alone. I wasn't sure if work was still my passion or just a distraction from the heavier things on my heart. I used to be so committed and passionate about my job. The next big idea was like an exciting safari hunt every day. I was driven and invigorated, but now it felt more like I was killing time, enduring the daylight simply to finally go home and escape to sleep. Nonetheless, days did go by and turn into nights.

Evenings with Spencer, homework, and then long nights of lying in the lonely darkness of our queen-size bed, which felt more like a football field with only me in it.

This day was the same. It transformed into evening, and it was time to head home. Everything felt numb again as I finished up my work. The magic of the day before had truly vanished like a sunset. I peeked over to check the time. Tonya's business card continued to taunt me from where I had laid it that morning. I looked at it again. Why didn't I just call? Was I going to carry the card around from work to home and back again in this continual, silly game?

I'm not sure if it was out of frustration or intrigue, but before I got up to leave, I picked up my office phone and began dialing. Then I hung up. What was I thinking? I paused, picked up the phone again, and dialed the entire number until it rang, but then quickly hung up again. *This is so stupid*, I thought as I used my good arm and one leg to lift myself from the office chair and head for the elevator.

That night was a long one. I felt the frustration of my loneliness. I was short with Spencer getting through dinner and homework and even shorter with myself getting into bed and trying to sleep. I still had pictures of Tamara all over the house like a shrine. I knew I'd never get over what happened. I felt like I was observing my brokenness without the courage to do anything about it. I just looked at the pieces but never attempted to see if the edges might match up somehow. I tossed and turned and simply waited for the alarm to sound as if that would grant permission for me to get up and start the whole routine over again. I'd get Spencer off to school and drag myself into the office to face another day. At least it hurried the hours along.

I arrived at work the next morning, took a deep breath, leaned back in my chair, and looked out my office window. I knew this was no way to live, yet no one could change it but me. I looked at the business card sitting where I left it and realized what a coward I was being. I read the name again: *Tonya Skubic*. It was time to do something, to move forward in some way. What did I have to lose?

I had already lost most of what mattered to me anyway. Without hesitation, I picked up the phone and dialed. It rang once, and my heart started pounding; twice, and I swallowed hard; three times, and I felt sweat form on my upper lip; and then a fourth ring. Finally, Tonya's voice sounded on the other end, but it was just her answering machine. *This is perfect*, I thought. *I can simply leave a message and not have to speak to her. Yikes, but what to say?*

After the beep, I said, "Hello, this is Jeff. We sat together at the luncheon this week at the New Yorker. By the way, this call has nothing to do with work. It's completely personal, but please call me back when you get a few minutes."

I hung up the phone, wiped the perspiration from my face with my hands, and then dried my hands on my jeans. I said it was personal, so she wouldn't return the call thinking it's business. Knowing it's personal, she'd only call back if she was interested, right? It's in her court.

I was talking to myself again. Why? That's when I realized what had happened, and what I had done. Did I actually make a phone call with the intention of asking this woman out? That felt strange. I thought of Tamara. *What was I doing?* Although she'd been gone over a year, calling another woman still felt so foreign to me.

I dove into my work and went on with the day. Before too long, however, Tonya actually called back, which caught me off guard. I didn't expect to hear back from her so quickly. Now I really was going to be forced to have the conversation rather than just fantasizing about how it might go.

"Hi, Tonya," I said. "Yes, it was fun. Thanks for calling back." My voice was obviously shaking. "Listen, you mentioned you'd found it difficult to meet people here and were leaving town. I get all that, but I was wondering. . . I mean, if you just want a friend or someone to hang out with, we could have dinner or something? I mean, I'm safe enough, and you're leaving anyway. I just thought, maybe, well, that we might at least enjoy each other's company. That's all. Would you join me Friday for dinner?"

I sat there, my heart pounding. I sounded so silly.

"Sure," she replied. "Where are we going? What shall I wear?"

I hadn't even gotten that far yet. "Pants or trousers will be fine," I replied. *What?* I thought, mortified. *Trousers. Listen to me. What am I even doing?*

"Okay. I'll just meet you at your office after work. I can be there by six."

"Perfect," I said and hung up the phone.

What was that? I couldn't believe what I had just done. It felt strange yet exciting, but it was mixed with tinges of guilt. I almost wanted to call back and say, "never mind. I was just kidding. I just wanted to see if I would really do it." But I knew I couldn't turn back now. I had taken what was a huge step for me, and the biggest miracle in all of it was that I actually picked up the phone to make the call. I was stunned and grateful, but scared.

CHAPTER 20

I woke up early Friday morning and took time to vacuum and clean up my truck. I arranged for the nanny to take Spencer to my mom's after school so I'd be free for dinner. The workday raced by, and soon it was time for my date. *Date?* I thought. *Am I crazy?* I watched out the window to see if Tonya would pull up, then I decided to go down to the parking lot to avoid having to use the big freight elevator in front of her. I was still a bit awkward on my leg and struggled to pull down the big metal doors with my shoulder in such a tender state. I left the building and limped toward my truck. I was ten yards from it when she pulled up in her car. I went numb.

"Hello," I heard myself say as she rolled down her window. I made my way around the truck to open the door for her while she parked and walked toward me. She got out of her car in one easy motion. She was strong and athletic but moved with a natural flow. She wore dark pants with heels and a simple, white button-up shirt and blazer on top. I didn't want to stare, but couldn't help notice every detail about her.

She exhibited the same grace as she jumped up into the passenger seat of my truck. I closed the door and limped to the driver's side, doing my best to get in effortlessly. I was worried and so self-conscious. I kept wondering what she was thinking, and then I worried again why it mattered. It didn't take long, however, until we were engaged in meaningful conversation as we drove up the canyon to a restaurant I loved.

It was rustic, yet lovely and quiet. The room was dimly lit, mostly by candles, and filled with the aroma of a natural wood fire mixed with the hint of the gourmet entrees as they came freshly prepared from the kitchen. Our table was near the fireplace, which crackled as we sat down. We were adjacent to a large picture window with a view of the few huge pine trees very near the restaurant. I noticed how the cool evening air danced in their big, waving bows. There was also a giant hand-woven Navajo rug on the far wall. I found myself taking it all in and beginning to actually get lost in rug's pattern rather than making conversation.

"The pepper steak here is awesome—if you feel like having steak twice in one week," I broke the silence as we settled in.

"Sounds good to me," she said.

"I'll ask the waiter to bring you some ketchup," I smiled.

She giggled, shrugged, and said, "I dare you."

She sat back in her chair to take off her jacket. Her blazer was purple. I noticed how she gracefully slipped it off and hung it on the chair behind her. I would have offered to assist her, but by the time I even thought it, the jacket was behind her and she was leaning back onto the table, resting her elbows on it with her chin on her hands.

She was beautiful. Her hair had a natural part in it and was held back with a small dragonfly hairpin. I noticed how tastefully she had applied conservative makeup simply to highlight her eyes and lips. Somehow the way she leaned onto the table, giving me her undivided attention, and the fact that she was already comfortable enough to slip off her jacket, put me so much at ease.

We ordered, and, yes, I even asked for a side of ketchup, which got a strange look from the waiter, but he brought it all the same. The conversation continued easy and unforced. She asked all the questions about the accident and what had happened. She asked about Spencer and how he was coping. I was able to maintain my composure and carry on an intelligent conversation, which actually surprised me, given I had held so much in for so long.

I kept having the strangest pings of emotions again as we sat talking.

The butterflies in my stomach were stabilized by a comforting warmth. I was able to open up as if I already knew her well. She was a good listener. I poured out many of my feelings about what had happened and what I had experienced. She had no judgment of any of it. She just listened. I shared personal insights and things I had learned over the past year.

I got a little emotional talking about the car crash but was even able to share some of that without hesitation. We eventually lightened the subjects and laughed a little together about work and current events. Even with the steady conversation, I still felt awkward at times, as if I was doing something wrong. I kept looking over my shoulder. I hadn't dated really at all, and it felt like I was stepping out on my wife or something. Even though Tamara had passed, I always considered myself a married man—until now.

As the night rolled on, I had the strongest feelings of love—yes, love—come over me. Not a romantic love, but a spiritual, unconditional love.

I had experienced something similar shortly after the accident happened. I had seen into people's souls, really feeling them and knowing them to the core. Now here I was, experiencing the same thing with this beautiful woman as we ate dinner and talked.

None of these emotions made sense. Why could I feel such deep, strong feelings for a stranger? I paused as it rushed over me. It began to frighten me, actually. I resolved that I must see a counselor or psychiatrist soon. How could I be feeling this, these strong rushes of love on the first date? I know I'm losing it, I decided as we finished our entrees and ordered dessert.

As the night continued, I was startled at how comfortable I became. We talked about many things in depth. We discussed religion and the role it had played in our lives. Tonya was a Catholic girl from Minnesota, but had spent half of her time growing up in the Bible Belt of Oklahoma. I was a Mormon from a dairy farm in a small town in the Utah mountains. We talked about our immediate and extended families and the backgrounds we came from.

Tonya also came from dairy farmer stock in Northern Minnesota, something we had in common. She was the oldest of three in her family and was quite close to her siblings, especially her younger sister, Tricia. We even talked about football and what was going on in the NFL that season. Mostly, we talked about spiritual things. I opened up enough to share some of the profound out-of-body experiences I had after the accident and during my time in the hospital.

I was actually enjoying myself and enjoying Tonya's company. It felt good to share so openly with someone outside of my immediate family and close work friends. The only uncomfortable aspect of the situation was, oddly enough, my comfort. My mind didn't know how to take it. I felt bad that I felt good, and yet I didn't want it to end.

By the time I dropped Tonya off and headed for home, it was way too late to pick up Spencer. I called my mom and asked if he could just spend the night with her and I would pick him up in the morning. As I reached over to grab my cell phone I realized I was still wearing my wedding band. That smothering, doubtful feeling started setting in again. My mom was still awake and picked up the call.

"Hi Mom. Sorry it's so late. I'm glad you're still up, though. Is Spencer doing ok?"

"He's already sound asleep, and it's perfectly fine," my mom replied. "How did things go?"

I didn't know what to say, and I didn't want to talk about it. I was confused by the joy and excitement of the experience mixed with a heavy dose of guilt. "Fine," I said and changed the subject. "I'll see you in the morning, Ma. Let Spencer sleep in, and I'll be by around ten."

Sitting in the silence of the ride home, I became a bundle of nerves and emotions. Why did I feel the way I did? By the time I got home I was a wreck. My eyes were wet with tears over the grief of losing my wife and youngest son. And now, I was out gallivanting with strange women and feeling all kinds of love-like emotions. I couldn't decide whether that was bad or good.

When I got home I made my way up the stairs and collapsed on my bed in a heap of private tears. "Help me, God," I uttered between sobs. "I don't know what's wrong with me, but I'm sure I'm losing my mind. I went out to dinner with a woman." I blurted this out, as if God didn't know already. "And I enjoyed it, but I'm really going crazy because I kept feeling love—like real love—for her, and I don't even know her. Help me, Father. I'm afraid I need a shrink. I miss Tamara so badly, and it hurts so deeply, yet tonight I felt happy. I felt love all around me. I . . ."

I rolled onto my back and took a deep breath. I felt the hot tears roll from the corners of my eyes and down into my ears. Then I heard it, not in my head, but in the core of my soul. I heard that still, small voice that spoke to the heart, and it said in a plain and powerful way, "The love you're feeling is not your love; it's my love for her."

I lay there on my back, catching my breath. I wiped the tears from the sides of my face. *His love for her?* Wow. Maybe that's why it feels so wonderful.

CHAPTER 21

I AWOKE WITH A START. It was strange to wake up to an empty house. *Spencer!* I thought. *My son.* I needed to check on him so I quickly stood, steadied myself on the bed, and picked up my phone to call my mom. The display read 6:32 a.m. They wouldn't even be up yet.

I sat back down and rubbed my eyes. Why was I so jittery? I replayed the events of the night before. They all felt a bit like a dream as I grabbed my crutches and made my way to the shower. Trying to go back to sleep was useless. I continued to replay the events of the previous night as the hot water raced over my body. How Tonya looked, what she said, how nice it was to share conversation like that.

I got out of the shower and grabbed a pair of comfortable jeans and my favorite pearl-snap button shirt. As I dressed and prepared to put the leg back on, I realized this new routine was never going away. No matter what I felt the night before—love, comfort—this routine of putting on the leg would always be painful and might cause bitter reflections.

I'll never forget, I thought as I pulled my stump into the cold, hard socket. The process existed so I'd always remember what I had and what I lost. Guilt plagued me again as I recounted the events of the previous night. What am I doing? I secured the leg on tight with the suction valve, pulled up my jeans, and took the phone from my pocket—7:22 a.m. I still had over two hours before I had to pick up my son, but there was something I knew I wanted to do first.

The sun was in full view over the eastern hills as I drove down Bountiful Boulevard to the cemetery where Tamara and Griffin were buried. My thoughts rushed to my grief again, and I fought back tears while I parked the truck, grabbed my cane, and made my way down the grassy hill to their markers. They had been buried on the south end of the cemetery near a lovely little evergreen. I stayed focused on the tree as I made my climb down the hill. Uneven terrain was the most difficult to navigate with the prosthetic leg.

By the time I arrived, the tears could be controlled no longer. They rushed freely down my face as I collapsed on the grave of my deceased wife and son. My body heaved as I poured out my soul into the cold, wet grass. "I don't know what I'm doing, Tam. I went on a date last night with a woman named Tonya. I'm sorry. I miss you so badly! I love you. Please come back to me somehow. I can't do this anymore."

I banged my head on the grass and wiped my eyes. I realized what I must've looked like, although no one was around to see me. I envisioned myself, a crippled man face down on the ground, sobbing over the grave of his loved ones. I composed myself long enough to sit up and look at the grave markers. Tamara and Griffin were really gone. The names and dates stared back at me with the same metallic coldness they were engraved in.

I wiped my eyes and found my way to my knees. Getting up was always awkward with one leg. I looked up at the sun, now gleaming down from behind light, wispy clouds. What was I going to do? How could I ever survive this? I could never love again, at least not like I had. But, at only thirty-five, the thought of remaining single the rest of my life seemed quite bleak.

I struggled to my feet and hobbled back to the truck. I drove down the small residential streets of the foothills and onto the interstate, heading south toward my mom's house. I didn't play the radio,—deep in thought. Was I being selfish? Was I motivated only by loneliness? Why did I feel so guilty about it? Yet even in the guilt and confusion, I wanted to see Tonya again. None of it made sense. We had so little in common. I was a Mormon from Utah, and she was a Catholic from Minnesota who would soon be leaving town.

When I arrived at my mom's, she was putting the customary big breakfast on the table: bacon, eggs, pancakes, and orange juice. Spencer was up and watching cartoons in the living room while his grandma cooked. I hurried in to him and gave him a big hug. The tears almost returned as I held him and wondered if I was betraying him too somehow. His cheerful mood kept my feelings in check and assured me he was fine.

He loved sleeping over at Grandma's and seemed unconcerned with my absence. We all ate together and only discussed the drawings my mom and Spencer had done together and the card games they had played. My mom must have sensed my unwillingness to talk about the events of the night before and held her questions for a more private time.

I was afraid to speak about my date, yet not an hour passed that I didn't think about how good it felt to be with someone and have meaningful conversation. But what of the strange, strong love I had felt sitting across the table at dinner and the whisper that had come to me when I asked God why?

I wanted to call Tonya again, to reach out and feel that love all over again. I wanted to laugh and watch her put ketchup on her steak, but I was still concerned that I was now a puppet in a crazy, self-created illusion of mine.

CHAPTER 22

I WAS LOST IN MY thoughts throughout the next day. Spencer and I went through our regular Sunday routine. We slept in a little later and had breakfast together at the small kitchen nook table. I played music on the stereo loud enough to fill the house with beautiful tones. He was happy, but had no idea what emotions I was experiencing. He hadn't even asked where I'd been two nights ago. I didn't tell him. I was so torn about how much to share with him.

He was just a little boy. He had experienced enough hurt and confusion in his life already. My job as his dad was to provide some stability, something he could count on. I wondered what that might look like in the future. Was I really protecting him by keeping it just the two of us? Would a woman in our lives just complicate things more? I knew I could never replace his mom, but he deserved a mother's love. And I deserved a woman's love as well.

After breakfast, we got dressed in Sunday jackets and ties and made our way to our chapel, which was just down the street. I didn't even speak to anyone in our congregation when we got there. I was stuck somewhere between feeling selfish and totally intrigued with what I had experienced on my date with Tonya. I wondered what people would think.

Would family and friends feel it was too soon for a relationship and that I should give things more time, or would they be glad I was trying to move forward? My mind was an endless blog of what-ifs that really didn't matter at this point. So, what? I went on a date and felt something. At least I could feel. Yes, it was causing all kinds of ping-pong feelings, but at least I knew I was alive.

Monday came, and the workweek rolled in. Spencer and I returned to our regular schedule of school, homework, and the nanny taking care of things until I got home. The urge to call Tonya continued, and I easily gave into it. It wasn't even lunchtime before I called her and arranged to meet that night for a few minutes after I finished at the office. With Spencer at home, I got creative about how to ease him and Tonya into things. I didn't feel comfortable springing her on him, or him on her for that matter. I wasn't sure about how far to take things with Tonya leaving.

Nonetheless, Tonya and I met almost daily after that. We would make plans for lunch or play a quick game of pool in the pub below my office after work. Mostly we just talked—usually long, late-night phone conversations after Spencer had gone to bed. I planned to introduce her to him when it made sense. I just wasn't sure how to do so, and whether the timing would ever be right.

What would I say? "This is the woman I'm eating dinner with sometimes and talking to on the phone"? or "Meet my new girlfriend; she's leaving in a month, so we're just having fun"? None of it made sense. And I was still far from being over my grief of losing Tamara and Griffin. All I knew was that I appreciated the company and wasn't willing to let it go.

I worried at times that I might be simply filling the big void within myself. I didn't want to play games with anyone, especially my son Spencer, but I felt compelled to see it play out. I knew Tonya would be leaving soon for Arizona and flirted with the notion that everything would simply come to an abrupt halt after she left. The thought hurt. The love I felt for her from the first date continued to grow. I was developing my own feelings independent of what I'd been told was "God's love for her."

Romantic urges were surfacing as well, which I had no idea what to do with. At times I felt selfish, and at others, I felt like this could be the perfect thing for Spencer. In the end, however, I knew I was falling in love, too hard and too fast, but somewhere in the free fall I felt joy. Healing was in Tonya's touch, her voice, and her laughter. Her energy filled me with excitement, but with a quiet comfort as well. I enjoyed being with her, even with all the mixed emotions it brought up.

In the process, I had actually decided to remove the wedding band my late wife Tamara had given me. I was indeed single, even if I still grieved the loss of my first marriage. The night I took it off was a painful one; it was like losing another part of me in many ways. I kept it in a small box in my nightstand with other things I counted as sacred. I knew the ring was just a symbol, and taking it off was a symbol of being open to other possibilities, including what doors might open since the ones I had adored for so long were now shut.

I eventually invited Tonya to our house. I wasn't sure what to do, however; I still had photos of Tamara and our family in almost every room. Should I take them all down, or would that only be fooling Tonya—and myself—that I was truly moving forward when I was really still grappling with many of my feelings? I wondered if I was only leaning into my relationship with Tonya knowing she was leaving soon. Was it just a false deadline with nothing beyond that?

Everything was becoming complicated. I wasn't sure whether Tonya was a mask to my pain or my deliverance from it. Was I only searching for what I'd lost, or was the true answer to joy right there before me? I didn't know, but I wanted to keep letting her in. I wanted her even closer. In my deepest heart, I didn't want her to leave so soon. I wanted time, time to see what played out and how I could eventually feel, but I wasn't sure how to ask for that. I knew, however, that I could only take one step at a time, the first being to invite her to our house and eventually introduce her to Spencer.

I decided to leave the photos up. I had nothing to hide. Many of our conversations had already revolved around the accident and my loss, but I hadn't revealed to Tonya all that I was going through emotionally with my newfound feelings for her. I felt she also wanted to meet Spencer, but I didn't want to confuse him by bringing a woman into our picture yet. Why introduce him to Tonya when I knew she was leaving anyway? It felt better to keep my relationship with Tonya from him for now. I didn't want to tear his emotional wounds open or cause him to think I was moving forward and leaving him behind in some way. I arranged for him to visit his cousins the night Tonya came over to simplify things.

Tonya came to the house. I had cleaned it well, but I left everything just as it had been. Tonya noticed all the photos of my late wife, my late son, and the entire family as soon as she came through the front door. It must have been quite weird for her. I had frames highlighting memories of a ten-year marriage in almost every room.

I had too much respect for Tamara to remove the photographs for a woman that was leaving town in two weeks. Yet in some strange way, I felt like I was actually introducing Tonya to the entire family through the photos. It was a bit psychotic, I know, but it seemed almost natural given the state I was in.

Tonya looked at many pictures of Spencer, and the conversation quickly turned to him.

"Do I get to meet him?" Tonya asked.

"Soon," I replied.

The question threw me, so I guided Tonya to the kitchen where we could escape the gaze of the photos for a while. I didn't want to tell Tonya that my intention was to wait until things got serious before I introduced her to Spencer. Would he think I was replacing his mother? I also didn't want Tonya to feel pressured since she would be leaving town anyway.

I purposely left all the other doors to rooms in the house closed. I knew if Tonya caught a glimpse of Tamara's sweater still lying over the chair next to my bed, she would really know how shattered I was. A rush of uncertainty about everything I was doing came over me again. I had such a hole in my heart to fill, and I knew no one could ever fill it. Still, I just wanted to be normal again. I wanted to feel like a whole man, and, somehow, Tonya had brought a taste of that. Her intense interest in me, along with her acceptance of my brokenness, brought me peace and courage.

CHAPTER 23

ALL OF THE EMOTIONS swirling around in the whirlwind of my and Tonya's relationship had begun to overwhelm me. She was leaving and I didn't want her to go. I wanted her to meet my son, but I didn't want to complicate things. Time and good judgment had lost all relevance. I was already in way too deep, even in the short few weeks we had spent together. I loved Tonya from the first time I saw her dipping her steak in ketchup. I would have never even called her had I not been overrun with such promptings from the beginning.

And the more time we spent together, the deeper the feelings grew. It felt natural but foreign to me. We drew clear lines about the physicality of our relationship, so why was I ashamed? I had been widowed for well over a year. I realized how starved I was for affection, yet I also realized that over those many months, I felt as if I was still married. I had never let go of Tamara. But Tonya's affection unlocked the human part of me that was a lonely man, something that I had kept in chains for so long.

Guilt only crashed its waves against what felt magical to me. How could I be in love with and grieving the wife of my youth while craving the new woman in my arms? The polarity of my feelings confused me. My heart expanded and divided between the wife I loved and lost, and the woman who had miraculously appeared in my life.

Overwhelmed with conflicting feelings, I headed to my place of comfort. Once again, I found myself in the cemetery on Tamara's grave, sobbing in a heap. It was early morning again, with no one around, but I didn't care who saw me. It was time to finally let go and address all that was in my heart. I wondered if Tamara could hear me. Was I praying to her or for her? I wasn't sure, but the purity of my emotions came flowing through the sobs:

"I'm having feelings for another woman, Tam. I don't know what to do. Please forgive me. I can't live without you, but I don't know how I'm going to do this. I feel so ashamed, yet happy at the same time. Please help me. Please guide me. I'm so worried about Spencer."

My deepest desires wept out onto the cool grass around the graves. I grieved openly in an honest confession about everything I was experiencing.

I was there for some time, gasping out my deepest fears and desires. I could barely see through my swollen eyes when I sat up and looked at the markers. I took in their names, the dates, and rubbed my fingers over the raised, bronze letters. All the pain of what had happened rushed over me. They were gone and I would never be the same.

"Tam," I whispered under my breath, "I really need you." But the stillness in the air reminded me of just how alone I was. I felt another hot tear well up, and it fell on the headstone right by Tamara's name. As I watched it dry in the sun, I felt a numbness start at the top of my head and travel down to the base of my spine.

Warmth engulfed me. My entire frame felt like it was vibrating, and everything around me became crystal clear. Heat penetrated into my shoulders and neck. A familiar energy settled right between my shoulder blades, and that's when I knew Tamara was there with me. I felt her love and spirit as real as if she had walked up behind me. I turned toward her and saw nothing, and when I reached out to touch her I felt nothing, yet I knew she was there. I could never forget her touch and the feeling Tamara brought with her whenever she was near.

I struggled to my feet and felt as if she actually embraced me. The experience was so real it was undeniable. I felt her arms around my neck and her body close to mine even though I could not see her. Pure intelligence rushed into my heart. Her voice spoke to me in the same tones it had when she was alive.

"My Jeff, you silly goose," Tamara said lovingly. "You may choose whomever you want? My deepest desire is for you to be happy and not alone. Your joy is my joy, and your pain is my pain. We are linked in death, but please know this: I sent Tonya to you. That's why you've had all the feelings you've been experiencing. The first time you saw her, all the déjà vu, even your romantic urges; they were all messages from me. I can do that from here. It is not only my right, but my privilege. There is only wisdom and love here. No jealousy, judgment, or possession. I wanted you to learn this, so I sent Tonya to you. She will teach you unconditional love. And that—in spite of all you've been through and learned—is the one thing you still get to work on: unconditional love."

As I felt her words, my surroundings seemed to disappear and I stood in a magical realm of light. I saw a vivid picture of a small pebble hitting a smooth surface of water, as if it were right in front of me. The ripples fanned out in eternal waves.

"Do you see what you have the opportunity to create here?" Tamara whispered to me. She repeated the same phrase I had heard right after our accident when my spirit left my body for a brief moment in time:

"To what degree have you learned to love?"

I stood there, feeling the sun on my face as I let the tears fall freely onto my chest.

"Stay with me, Tam. I want you here."

"Choose joy," she reminded me, as I had been told before. I felt her leaving.

"Don't go," I begged. "Please!"

But the reality of her fading away reinforced the fact that she had literally been with me.

I had an answer. The words "choose joy" echoed in my heart. I had been given those words during one of the darkest nights of my soul. I cried out to

God and asked why all this had happened to me and how I would I ever make it. "Choose joy," was the answer then, and again now. I knew my next step.

I resolved to love Tonya without any shame or guilt. She was what I wanted, and I had received so many spiritual insights. I knew she was a gift from above. The bottom line was quite plain: I had fallen in love with her. It didn't need to be any more complicated than that. Love was reason enough to let down my walls and finally begin to choose joy.

CHAPTER 24

"I'M LEAVING NEXT WEEK for Tempe," Tonya said without hesitation as we talked on the phone. I had a break in my workday and decided to call her. She continued, "My sister will meet me there in a month or so. I want to find an apartment and get all set up before she comes. I've already accepted my new job. I just have to figure out how to get all my stuff moved down there. I think I'll hire a moving company to haul it for me once I know where I'll be."

It hit me like a brisk crosswind. The time had passed so quickly. "Wow," I said. "It's here already isn't it?"

"Yes," she agreed. "I can't see you this weekend. I'm loading the bare necessities into my car and heading out Friday. My last day on the job here in Salt Lake is Wednesday."

"Do you have time for lunch on Wednesday? I'd like to see you before you go."

"Of course. I'll make time."

I hung up and looked at the clock on my office wall. Maybe I had been wrong, but I was sure it wasn't just my imagination at the gravesite. Tamara had spoken to me, and everything I had experienced up to this point was pointing to Tonya. She had magically shown up in my life, and now she was leaving just as quickly as she had appeared.

I hurried through my work and headed home.

My mom was watching Spencer that day because the nanny had taken a long weekend trip with friends. When I arrived home, my mom had done the laundry and was just folding the last batch of whites to put in my dresser. I could smell dinner in the oven, and Spencer was happily painting pictures at the kitchen table. Thank goodness for moms.

We ate together, cleaned up, and then talked and laughed while we worked on one of those silly three-dimensional puzzles of a human face Spencer had gotten for his birthday some months before. There was such peace in the house. I adored my mother for how supportive she was throughout the entire ordeal. After Spencer had gone to bed, my mom lingered to talk as she methodically put the dishes into the dishwasher, and, as moms often do, she asked all the questions about Tonya and what was happening in my life.

I answered with short, vague answers until I realized she had finished loading the dishwasher as slowly as she possibly could without me really telling her anything. I finally opened up as she picked up her purse to leave. I realized I didn't want her to go without sharing with her how I was feeling. We sat back down at the kitchen table as I told her what was happening to me: Tonya was moving to Arizona and I wasn't sure what to do. I didn't want to come off as a needy weirdo, I explained, but what could I say in this situation besides good-bye and good luck?

I paused. "I don't know why I want this so bad, Mom, but I do."

My mom's face was sober and empathetic, but her eyes seemed to smile as if she were happy that her son was actually feeling again. She got up from the table, hugged me, and simply reminded me that I had all my own answers as she grabbed her things and headed for her car.

I watched from the window while she drove away. I turned and headed up the stairs, using the handrail to do most of the upward pulling with my arms. Halfway up, I glanced back down at the spotless kitchen and listened to the dishwasher as it ran. It was nice to have my mom there.

A woman's touch had been nonexistent in our home. I missed the way

Tamara had always held the house together. I felt I was a good dad but, honestly, a pretty lousy mom. My heart ached for Spencer. Would he ever remember what it used to be like before the wreck, when his own mother was there? Would he ever forgive me for the trauma the accident had put him through?

I pulled myself the rest the way up the stairs and made my way to the bed to take off my prosthetic leg. *Would I ever feel whole again? Was I simply flattered that a beautiful young woman had actually taken interest in me? And had she, really, or was this all an illusion in my own mind?*

The quiet of the loneliness closed in on me as I lay on the bed and shut my eyes. Should I call Tonya and tell her not to leave? Should I ask her to stay here with us and see what we might create together? Maybe I was just holding her captive in my pain when she could be free to find her own joy.

"Guide me, Lord," I said in a quiet prayer. "Don't let my imagination or my heart run away with me. Grant me the wisdom to do the best thing."

But what if Tonya didn't feel the same? She had never once brought up an alternative to leaving for Arizona to meet her sister and start fresh there. I also knew I was still grieving. I was so broken in many ways that it frightened me. I didn't want Tonya to know about all the doubt mixed with the love I was experiencing. And if she knew how broken that made me feel, could she ever really love me?

I finally slipped into a light, restless slumber with that burning question still on my mind: *did she love me?* The question was coupled with the worry of what was next and what was best for my son. The confusion was as smothering as the thick, bulky comforter on the bed. I stirred just long enough to throw the down comforter aside and lie in the coolness of the breeze coming in from the open window.

CHAPTER 25

I AWOKE WITH THE RESOLVE that I would not just let Tonya go without telling her how I felt. The stirrings were deep, and she deserved to know my heart even if my feelings were only one-sided.

We met for lunch at a quaint cafe downtown. Tonya was casual with her hair pulled back in a baseball cap and ponytail. She had been packing for her move. I was in my typical jeans, t-shirt and a jacket, since I didn't have any business meetings that day. The situation already seemed strange. I didn't know how to approach the subject, so I just blurted it out over the awkward small talk of her moving plans.

"What if you didn't go?" I asked suddenly. "What if you just stayed here and we saw how things might play out between us? The truth is, I don't want you to go. I want you to stay here."

She paused. The silence was too long, but then she giggled nervously a little and moved onto more small talk of when the moving company would be coming to pick up her furniture and if I could assist them with collecting it.

I wanted to shout, "Stop! No, you're not listening to me." I wanted to tell her that this had been plaguing me for weeks, and that I had actually broken down on my deceased wife's grave just days ago about my feelings for her and had an undeniable experience—but I didn't.

I still feared she would see me as some deranged man living in a fantasy of how I would put my life back together. Her body language and nervous response also gave me the clear signal that she wasn't interested in a conversation like that. So, I sat in silence just listening to her, feeling my head nod affirmatively that I would assist her with the moving company once she arrived in Arizona.

I felt like an idiot. *Why did I even ask?* I thought. *It's obviously too soon, and she barely knows me.* And why did I feel I had to force the issue anyway? Why couldn't I simply trust that angels were at work in my behalf and let things play out as they were intended to?

I sat there blushing and feeling silly as I sipped my water and avoided eye contact with Tonya. I didn't want my food. I felt like a politician simply agreeing and saying what I wanted her to hear. I watched myself commit to everything she was saying about getting out of town. I was ignoring all of my own feelings. Was this my only chance? No other woman would show interest in a one-legged man with a son. And I wanted her, not only because of the experience I had at the gravesite, but because I was in love with her.

Tonya finished her lunch while mine sat untouched on the plate since my question. We got up to leave, and I resolved that she was walking out of my life. What did I expect, really? None of this made sense, and the spiritual things I had been experiencing would never jive with the ego and natural progression of things.

Tonya left at the end of the week as planned. We had a long phone conversation as she drove. I pretended that I just wanted to make sure she arrived safely, but deep down it was my way of holding on for a little longer. The conversations continued nightly, but they were filled only with the details of her search for a new apartment, her new job, and the typical daily activities.

It took me by surprise when she announced that she would be coming back to Salt Lake for the weekend to tie up some loose ends here. I jumped at the opportunity and made plans immediately for her to spend time with us and meet Spencer. It was nice because it actually felt as if the pressure was off, somehow.

It had also given me a chance to look at things from a different perspective while she was away for two weeks. I had been so determined to make the relationship work that I had forgotten to simply trust the fact that the spiritual answers had already come. I had made a new commitment to let things be. Whatever was meant to turn out would, and there was no need for me to force things.

I felt much better; in fact, the message I had received at the gravesite to learn unconditional love made more sense now. I could love Tonya without stipulations of what our relationship should become or what it should look like. That changed my entire demeanor about us into something more natural and easy.

Tonya arrived on Friday evening and spent her entire Saturday with us. Her visit was delightful. She and Spencer got along splendidly. He was excited to meet her and took her for a short hike on the back hill behind our house after lunch to gather wildflowers. I watched as they made their way down the small game trail and through the oak and wild maples.

I hadn't realized how Spencer must have missed having someone to hike with. The back hill was far too steep for me to manage with my leg, and we hadn't been out on the hill since the accident had happened. He was giddy, pointing things out to her and being quite talkative. She laughed and conversed with him in a way that was beautiful. It was hardly fair to my heart to see them together like that. As they walked down on the lower trail, I saw Spencer reach over to take her hand, not to hold it but simply to pull her in another direction toward the south end of the lot where the larger maples grew.

When I saw him reach out to grab her hand, I experienced even deeper love for Tonya. In fact, she looked so much like Tamara in that moment as she walked with Spencer it almost startled me. It was the way her hair bounced as she laughed and how they interacted. Spencer was warm and uninhibited toward her. Tonya was comfortable, which caused my soul to smile. I watched from the deck and reminded myself to be cool and trust the process without putting any expectations on her or anything else. I simply watched and delighted in their happiness.

That night, we all played Yahtzee at the kitchen table and laughed together until our stomachs hurt. What was meant to be just one game turned into a best-of-three tournament that went well into the night. I don't even remember who won, and it didn't matter. There was no pressure about anything.

Later, after Spencer had actually gone to bed, Tonya explained that the relationship would really never work. She was now settled in Arizona, and she didn't want to give the wrong impression by being here. As odd as it was, it came as no surprise to me. I was calm and actually content. I smiled and simply rubbed her shoulder.

"I know," I said. "And thank you for today. It meant a lot to both of us."

She hugged me. I held her tightly. I really was okay with letting her go even though the day had been so awesome. It was so liberating that I didn't have to make something happen or devise a plan of action toward some desired ending. For all I knew, this was the end of our relationship, and I was at peace with it. I had no expectations and no desired outcome, simply gratitude for having peace in the present moment.

"Do me a favor," I whispered as I held her. "Don't forget how this feels, okay? No matter where life takes you and what you experience, remember how this feels."

She kissed me and said, "I will. I promise."

Saturday became Sunday, and I knew Tonya would be leaving again. She actually ended up coming to church with us. She had always wondered what a Mormon service must look like and decided to join us probably more out of curiosity than anything. It was like we just wanted to bask in the peace of the day before. Odd, but knowing it was over was almost magnetically driving us closer.

Even if we were just friends, it was another hour we could spend together before she flew away again. That time was calm and happy, and it was nice to have someone sit by me. She even sang the hymns, and I enjoyed listening to her voice. We drove her to the airport that evening, and Spencer chattered continually about the animal facts book he brought along. He told her about everything from how far whales migrate and the territory one mountain lion can cover to how much a chipmunk can carry in its mouth. Tonya listened patiently and laughed with Spencer until it was time to send her to the departure gate. We shared one last big hug and she was off.

She and I exchanged emails and talked over the phone on a daily basis. We couldn't seem to stay away. I had lots of frequent flyer miles saved up, and we often made silly wagers on the Yahtzee games we'd play at my table when she visited, Spencer included, which led to additional trips to Salt Lake. Every weekend she was with us seemed to end with a Saturday night Yahtzee game, the loser providing a ticket to the winner. I'd lose on purpose.

Our relationship continued to progress, and even though we had decided it would never work out, we seemed to be doing wonderfully. Months passed, all the while with Tonya visiting us in Salt Lake or me visiting her in Arizona, but we stayed connected. The long-distance relationship allowed us to connect on deeper levels. Without the physical proximity, we connected soul-to-soul, which was far more powerful than mere physical attraction.

The relationship had naturally developed into something quite beautiful, and it happened naturally without force or expectations. Eventually, Tonya sent me an email that asked, "Where is all this going?" What we had been so willing to let go of had developed into something neither of us wanted to be without. I knew it was in my court as to where to take next steps and to what level, but knowing Tonya was open to, maybe even hoping for, that kind of commitment created a space where I finally felt safe going.

CHAPTER 26

THE FIRST PERSON I consulted was my eight-year-old son. We had talked a lot about Tonya, and he enjoyed her visits. They had developed a relationship, but it was only so deep based on Tonya's brief weekend visits. Tonya and I had also discussed Spencer at length and what it all meant for her should we continue our courtship. The questions still had to be asked of him, however, and I knew this was as important to Spencer as it was to me. It's funny how simple his response was. Kids have a way of cutting to the chase and getting to clarity much quicker than we do: they speak truth.

"So, how would you feel if we had Tonya around more permanently?" I asked him as we drove in the truck to go visit family.

"That would be awesome, Dad, but what do you mean?" Spencer replied.

"Well, I mean like having her move back here to Utah," I tried to explain. "You know, giving her a reason to stay here."

"You mean like getting married?"

He said it; I didn't. "Yes, like getting married maybe."

"Well that's easy, Dad," Spencer said. "You just ask God if she's the right one, and he'll let you know in some way that she is."

Wow. It really was that simple. I felt I had already been given the answer months ago, yet here we were at the actualization of such a prospect.

Spencer was right: I already had my answer. At least he was supportive and not resentful about the possibility. The only missing key was that Tonya would have to say yes.

She was coming to Salt Lake again that weekend. I didn't want a fancy or cliché engagement, so I decided I would pop the big question in a unique and meaningful way.

It had been a bit of a whirlwind romance with airplane tickets and back-to-back weekend plans. I wanted to bring it all down to earth with a simple, real proposal. I wanted to show myself at the core of who I was. Bottom line: I'm a simple farm boy, so I decided to propose back on the farm I grew up on.

We had a lower pasture that ran along a small canal, which was only about a hundred yards from the upper Provo River. A bridge spanned across it, and I had sat there as a boy, dangling my feet and contemplating my life and dreams as I watched the current run powerfully and continuously under me. I decided that I would pop the question there, on that bridge where the energy of my authentic self resided and the hopes and dreams of my youth were born.

I had a small table set up on the bridge with a nice tablecloth on it, two chairs, and one single candle in the middle. There was a dirt lane leading to the bridge that would easily accommodate my truck. I could drive right to the bridge, sit Tonya at the table, and express my feelings. I wanted her to see past the advertising executive, the creative director, the widower, and see me: the simple farm boy who was striving to put a life back together not only for myself but also, more importantly, for my son.

I purchased a ring to make it all legitimate, and I knew enough of Tonya's taste to be confident it was what she wanted. I had actually had it designed and handmade by a jeweler friend from a sketch Tonya had made over a conversation we had had weeks earlier about the perfect ring. Everything was set up. I only had to pick Tonya up at the airport and ask the question.

Tonya's flight was delayed and she got in later than expected. The sun was down and it was already getting dark. The drive to the bridge was quiet.

I had only told her I wanted to show her something and left it at that. As we drove, the weather became stormy. A light rain was falling by the time we drove onto the old farmstead. I pointed out my childhood home, the big weeping willow tree, and the large red barn, as well as the rope swing we had played on as boys. It was strange to see it all now. It used to seem so massive, and yet it felt tiny as I showed Tonya. Maybe life had gotten much bigger, and that's why my childhood home felt so small.

As we made our way down the dirt lane, the rain worsened and fell quite heavily by the time I reached the bridge with the table and candle on it. Oddly enough, the candle still burned brightly in spite of the rain. It acted as a glowing beacon to guide our steps as we made our way to it. It was quite a sight to see that little, nicely set table on the old country bridge with the rain falling all around it.

The rain fell hard enough now that it splattered up as it hit the pooling ground. I grabbed an umbrella from the back of the truck and walked Tonya toward the table. I could sense her curiosity and her anticipation. I was cautious not to slip on what was becoming mud under our feet. Luckily for us, there were enough patches of grass to step our way to the wooden bridge without soiling our shoes terribly.

I sat her down under the umbrella, and with rain now running over my head and face, I told her how I felt and why I had chosen this humble setting to have the most important conversation of my life. The rain dripped down over my eyebrows and we laughed as I stooped from the chair and actually got down on one knee.

Then I asked the question: "Are you willing to not only be my wife, but to be Spencer's mother, too?"

I presented the ring in classic fashion and waited, soaked in rain, for her response. She actually giggled a little, and her laughter soon turned into tears as she said, "Yes! Of course, yes!" She sprung from the chair and assisted me to my feet. We hugged, laughing and crying. She put on the ring and we made our way back to the truck. As we looked back at the little table in the pouring rain, the candle still burned brightly.

"The storm can't seem to put it out," Tonya remarked.

"I know," I replied. "Strange, but it burns on, no matter what."

We watched as we drove back up the dirt lane, and the candle remained glowing until we had driven far enough that we could see it no more. Only the coming years would reveal how symbolic that little candle was.

CHAPTER 27

S PENCER WAS THE FIRST to see the ring and congratulate us both. He seemed a little apprehensive, however, at the reality of the ring on Tonya's finger. Even though he knew I was going to ask, the talk of wedding plans would still have to settle in a bit. He didn't ask many questions. He just said, "cool," and went back out to the trampoline to jump alone. Tonya watched him from the window for a while but eventually made her way down to join him.

I watched for a moment as they jumped together then went up to the bedroom to contemplate my son's emotions and how I might best manage them. I always left the bedroom window open, and I could hear Tonya and Spencer on the trampoline. Their laughter and conversation among the sound of the bouncing trampoline springs gave me some reassurance.

I sat in the chair in the corner of the room, realizing I had made the right choice, but had to handle a lot of emotions. I knew my neighbors and friends were all watching, and Tonya had stepped into the big shadow cast by Tamara's memory. It always becomes larger than life when someone dies. People seem to idealize the deceased in a way that becomes unrealistic. Tamara was a wonderful person and had shed her influence on so many in our community. To me, though, she was simply Tamara, a loving wife and mother who had left this world much too soon. I was doing all I could to create something peaceful for Spencer and me to capture that happiness and love we had lost.

I knew many would think I was remarrying too soon, and others would question my choice in Tonya. The community had eulogized Tamara in such a way that no one would ever fill her shoes. It bothered me. At one point, I even listed in my journal all of the little quirks and imperfections Tamara had just so I could remember the real her.

I jotted down the way she made endless lists of everything she wanted to accomplish day-to-day. She insisted that the toilet paper be hung so the end always fell down over the top of the roll and not be pulled from the bottom up. I even noted her endless commitment to never going to bed with dirty dishes in the sink, the notion that thank-you notes should always be sent out immediately and that a phone call or simply saying thank you, would not do. She called me Jeffery when I was in trouble, was an early morning person even on Saturday and wore socks to bed.

But that's who I had loved: the beautiful but normal, meticulous, yet down-to-earth woman with all the common, typical, little idiosyncrasies that people tended to forget when someone beloved dies.

I realized that the sound from the bouncing springs on the trampoline had ceased, but I still heard voices through the open window. I concentrated to listen.

"You know, Spence," Tonya said in a soft tone, "your mom and I made a deal a very long time ago in a different realm,"

I pulled my focus in even tighter to hear her continue.

"You were such an amazing boy that God decided we could share you," Tonya explained. "You were too good to leave to just one mom. Your first mom and I agreed that she would bring you into this world and get to be your mom through your early years, and then she would go back home, and I would get to be your mom as you grew into a man."

Spencer was silent. I could not see them on the trampoline in the darkness from my window, but I could feel the energy of the conversation, and it was good.

"You never have to forget or let go of your first mom. She loved you more than anything in this world. She'll always be watching over you. Think of me as your second mom. You'll have one here taking care of you and another up above looking out for us both every step of the way. Does that make sense?"

I stood to peek out the window and saw Spencer nodding his head.

"C'mon. Let's see who can jump highest!" Tonya exclaimed. She rose, took his hands, and they jumped together.

My heart filled with gratitude. The freshness of this wedding proposal and acceptance had made concrete something that had simply been a notion until shortly beforehand. The reality of something we want can often fill us with doubt and concern. I was aware of all I was taking on and the challenges that might come from it. Spencer was only eight, and even though this was all expected, it may have taken him by surprise to see it come to fruition. At least Tonya had clarity in that moment. I knew it was going to be alright. There were still lots of unanswered questions for all of us, but I knew if we kept things in perspective, the answers would surely come.

CHAPTER 28

THE FOLLOWING WEEKS AND months were filled with wedding plans and organization, which all took place long distance. Tonya was still committed to her employer in Arizona, and the wedding would take place in Minnesota where Tonya's family lived. I did all I could from Utah as we pulled together family and friends to assist us with the plans.

Spencer fell right in line with it all and agreed to be the ring bearer for the ceremony. Everything came together quickly and seamlessly, except for my insecurities. Our courtship had been traditional, and we had agreed to reserve intimacy until our wedding night. I was so concerned about my body. The scars and my missing limb filled me with anxiety. Tonya was such a beautiful woman, and I could hardly believe that she would choose me, but she had, and that alone gave me confidence to get over my fears of being too broken to love her madly.

The wedding was beautiful. The weather was warm for fall in Minnesota, and family and friends came from all over the country to support us and wish us well. It was an outdoor garden reception, and my bishop, the leader of my congregation, flew out from Utah to perform the services. Spencer was elated to be the ring bearer and even took the first dance with Tonya.

We honeymooned in Mexico, then moved rapidly forward into adapting to new things. Tonya did her best to transition from a single, carefree career girl to a full-time wife and mother. I agreed to remodel the house, allowing Tonya to make it her own. There were a lot of moving parts, and we all did our best to make it work. The transition to marriage was not without its challenges; two cultures were melding together, and we had to let go of many aspects as well as embrace new things.

Throughout our courtship I had slowly taken down pictures of Tamara and had put everything away long before Tonya ever moved in. That was an emotional process for me. I didn't want to feel like I was completely letting go, but I wanted to be fair to Tonya by not bringing my past into our new marriage. I experienced a true depth of her character one day when I noticed that Spencer had always kept a picture of his mom on his nightstand. As Tonya was cleaning one day, I noticed as she dusted the top of the nightstand and placed the photo back in place.

"I could ask him to put that away if it bothers you at all," I suggested.

"You will do no such thing," Tonya replied emphatically. "That is his mother. He deserves to always have a picture of her near him."

As Tonya set up house and created a beautiful home of her own, she actually set out another photo of Tamara and Griffin in the main hall of the house, where we had all kinds of personal photos from our lives displayed.

"You don't have to do that. It's okay," I commented.

"I know I don't have to. I've chosen to," She told me. "I'm not threatened by your past or even the love you have for your first wife. An accident happened and had it not; I wouldn't be here with you. As I witnessed you going through all the pain and knowing how much you hurt over the loss, I saw a man who could love. Knowing you had the capacity to love at that level was half the attraction in the first place. Otherwise, why would I have given in to a one-legged Mormon man with a son? I had other options, you know."

She moved close and hugged me tight and kissed me on the cheek.

"It's okay," she continued, "I want the pictures up. It's a part of you. It's a part of Spencer, and now it's a part of us." She paused, looking warmly at me, assuring me with her eyes that all was well. I felt much better, but wondered if I expected her to be jealous and possessive of me. Was I being selfish in feeling that way? Tonya was magnificent in her maturity about the situation, perhaps more than myself.

The months rolled on and things began to settle in. Spencer was doing well, and we were making our new family work. I won't pretend it was easy; Tonya had taken on a lot coming into the situation cold turkey. Managing the house and the homework was, in and of itself, a full-time job—not to mention taking care of me. I had ongoing health issues, which included everything from infections in my leg to stomach and lung setbacks from the original injuries sustained in the crash.

None of it was incapacitating. I continued working, but frequent visits to the doctor and even the emergency room were a common occurrence. My body was still healing and, in many ways, so was my heart. I still had pain over the loss of my wife and child. Tonya could not heal those. In many ways, it was unfair for me to expect she would. It was joyful having her in my life, but she could not heal my heart—only a lot more time and myself could do that. I would never get over what had happened, but I was working on getting used to it.

Tonya had settled in as Spencer's caregiver in wonderful ways. She was naturally a good mother. And, though it had its challenges as well, her nurturing instinct was taking over and making a huge difference in his well-being. I could tell that Tonya could see the difference she was making, and I believe she found satisfaction in it. She even began discussing the notion of having more children. This took me by surprise since we had always just spoken in the realm of Spencer. In fact, Tonya already explained that she had experienced enough serious female issues in her adult life that doctors informed her that she might not have the ability to get pregnant.

I was perfectly fine with that since we already had Spencer. However, Tonya was very interested in having more children. Knowing her own medical issues, she was leaning toward adopting. She felt an intense urgency to add children to our fledgling family. I was reluctant since we were still working on our relationship and Tonya was still bonding with Spencer. It felt too soon to me, but her feelings would not go away.

She kept having intense, reoccurring dreams. In the first dream, her grandmother, who had recently passed away, came to our home driving a big, black limousine. Tonya found this odd since her grandmother was a hardworking and down-to-earth person, a nurse, and the wife of a dairy farmer in Northern Minnesota.

She pulled up to the curb and started to unload the limo, which was full of baby supplies: diapers, cribs, high chairs, toys, blankets—everything anyone would ever need to care for a baby. Her grandmother did not speak, but continued to unload all of the baby gear as she smiled pleasantly at Tonya.

In another dream, Tonya heard a knock at the door. As she opened it, she recognized the man standing there as my deceased business partner. She had never met him but recognized him from photographs I had displayed both at home and at the office. He had been killed in an airplane accident one year before I lost Tamara and Griffin. He was young, only twenty-nine. We had been good friends and had become close through working together to start our own advertising agency. He too didn't say a word in the dream, but smiled pleasantly and handed Tonya a brown paper grocery bag, which he had folded over at the top. She unfolded the top of the bag and looked at the contents. It was full of baby clothes. She gasped and looked up at him, but he was gone.

In a third dream, Tonya was at the airport anxiously awaiting the arrival of an airplane. She watched, waiting for her expected passenger even though she wasn't sure who it was. She observed passengers coming off the plane, looking closely for the friend she was anxious to meet; however, she wasn't clear on who that friend was. Suddenly, a thin blonde woman about her size rushed toward her with open arms and hands full of shopping bags. She knew immediately that it was Tamara, my deceased wife, whom she also had never met but recognized from photographs. They embraced, and Tonya felt a deep kinship with her. Not a word was spoken in this dream either, but the shopping bags were handed over, and again as Tonya opened them, they were filled with wonderful items for babies.

Tonya kept telling me of her strong feelings and dreams, which she knew came from inspiration. I listened intently and wondered about all of it. I knew the power of dreams and messages but was hesitant to adopt so soon. Honestly, I was fearful that I might feel differently toward adopted children. Perhaps I would love them less than my natural son. The whole idea filled me with anxiety, but Tonya was persistent.

CHAPTER 29

O NE EVENING AS I returned home from work, Tonya explained
that she had made an appointment with an adoption agency and
wanted me to attend with her for an orientation meeting.

"There's no pressure," she continued. "They'll simply walk us through
the process and show us how it all works."

I figured there was no harm in being informed, so I agreed to attend
the meeting. When we arrived, there were several couples there. All of them
were desperate to adopt. In fact, some of them had waited childless for years.
Tonya and I both felt a little sheepish being there since we had Spencer and
had only been trying to get pregnant for a few months now.

Nonetheless, we listened as they explained the adoption process. Each
couple was to submit a portfolio, though many had already done so, and
there were several examples for us to review at the meeting. The portfolios
were beautiful with pages of photographs, family histories, and detailed
explanations of family traditions. They included memories and intended
details of what couples wanted to create with their child should they be
considered and selected as an adoptive family. The portfolios would be
shown to the potential birth mothers, who would select the couple or family
they desired their child to be placed with.

Again, I found it odd that we were there, but we filled out a guest log with our names and contact information and stayed for the entire meeting. We saw the heartbreak of these individuals as they shared how desperately they wanted to have children and could not. We left with the resolve that we could wait, but Tonya still had the nagging feeling that it was what we were meant to do.

Less than a week later, I was in my office one morning going over email and preparing for the day when I received a phone call from the adoption agency. They asked how interested we were in adoption. When I asked why, the man on the other line described the situation: "We have a birth mother that arrived here this morning. She has a toddler, just over a year old, and is pregnant with a son due this fall. She wants the brothers to stay together in the same family."

The word "toddler" grabbed my heart; I thought of Griffin at the time of the accident. Also, the statement about "brothers staying together" got my attention based on my relationship with my own brothers. The emotions flooded over me as I recalled all of Tonya's impressions and her conversations over the past several weeks. Somehow, I knew these were my sons coming to me. A rush of warm energy bloomed as I felt the essence of what was being explained.

"Why did you call us?" I asked quite hesitantly, as if I already knew what was coming.

"Well, this may or may not sound odd to you, but as an adoption agency staff, we are committed to placing these children in the correct families," the agent explained. "Quite honestly, Mr. Olsen, we pray together as a staff each morning, and as we did so today, we were all overwhelmingly impressed upon to contact you. Of course, the birth mother will make the final selection, and she already has eleven portfolios to review, but if you'd like to be considered, I suggest you get your portfolio down here immediately."

"We don't have a portfolio at this point," I replied, "but I will contact Tonya and get you something as soon as possible."

I called Tonya and asked if she was sitting down.

"Yes," she answered. "Why, did they call?"

"Yes, in fact they did. And they want us to get them some materials right away to be considered by a birth mother today."

"I knew it!" Tonya replied. "I've been feeling it all morning. I knew something was up."

Tonya quickly hand-scrawled a letter and selected a few snapshots to put in an envelope. That would have to be our portfolio at this point. It was all we had time for, and might have seemed quite quaint among all the other beautiful portfolios. But something told me this was meant to be and that these boys were coming to our home.

Sure enough, we got a call from the adoption agency later that afternoon informing us that the birth mother had selected us as the family she wanted both her sons placed with. The counselor explained that as soon as she opened the letter and saw the photos, she began to tear up. Even among all the wonderful portfolios, she just had a feeling about us, and after reading Tonya's letter, she knew we were the ones. She insisted that she meet us first in person, though, just to be sure she was making the right decision.

We agreed to meet her the next day and, after a short visit, it was decided that we would meet Zach, her fourteen-month-old son, the next day at the zoo. It was a beautiful, clear day. Spencer came as well. Zach was already toddling about and was big for fourteen months. When we sat down, he actually climbed off of his birth mother's lap and went directly to Spencer.

Although Zach didn't talk at that point, he laughed and gave Spencer a hug, then started doing a sort of stomping dance in front of him. When he made his way to me, he actually put his hands on my face and said plainly, "Dad." I held him for a while as he patted my cheeks and played with my face, and then I handed him to Tonya. He was as comfortable in her arms as anything. He lay his head on her chest and started to stroke her wavy, strawberry-blonde hair.

That pretty much sealed the deal. I felt the love and the energy of that little boy as he came into our life as a gift. Tonya had been right; we were meant to adopt, and ready or not, we had two more sons coming.

The birth mother seemed relieved and resolved to take the next steps.

She was healthy and far along with the other upcoming baby boy. We felt his presence as well and knew the two were meant to stay together and be with us. By the next day, the agency was working with a district judge to get the paperwork together and the due diligence and background checks done. The adoption proceedings were under way.

The legal details were handled quickly, and soon the day came for Zach to come home with us. The birth mother wanted to actually give Zach directly to us. We were happy to accommodate her wishes to make the process easier for her. We had become aware of her deep love for her children. Her intention was not to "give them up" but to give them something better. This was the most selfless act I had ever seen anyone perform. It was not easy for her at all.

We sat for nearly five hours as she mustered the courage to pass him to me. It was heart wrenching. I kept telling her we didn't have to go through with it. We could simply all go home and forget it ever happened, but she insisted that it was meant to be. She said she knew the boys belonged with us. I knew the pain of losing a child, As well as the agony of handing a child over to someone else. I had experienced that shortly after the accident in a profound dream about my son Griffin. What we were experiencing with this young mother was no less poignant than that dream, and it was now playing out in reality.

Eventually, Zach fell asleep. While he slept, his mother was able to kiss him on the face and hand him to me. I had a vivid flashback from my dream when I had handed Griffin over to God. I felt such responsibility as I took my new son in my arms. I had been right there when the doctor delivered my other two boys, and this was no less sacred than when I took each of them into my arms for the first time.

I felt the mother's pain in letting go, and her trust and confidence in us becoming the parents of her child. It was overwhelming. Tears ran freely down all of our faces as the exchange was made. We committed to be in close contact with her until her unborn son came, and even beyond if she wished to.

The unconditional love we witnessed in her willingness to provide a better opportunity for her children above her own feelings was beyond words: that was love at the deepest level. I had experienced that in the dream with my son Griffin, passing him over to what I knew was a greater good and higher cause. But my heart went out to this young mother, having had not only the empathy of losing a child but also knowing what it felt like to give away a part of you that you love so deeply. I wept openly, holding Zach as she gathered her things and left the room to be alone and grieve.

CHAPTER 30

Zach was now home. The love I felt for him was as strong as anything I had ever experienced with my own natural sons. My fears were soon alleviated as I realized that he was my boy. He had just come in a different way, but he was as much mine as my other sons.

There were still a lot of things to handle and adjustments to make. Spencer was key in grafting him in. They would play loud music and dance together, giggling until they were so exhausted they would just lie still on their backs, resting for a few minutes before they started the whole ritual over again with a new song.

The birth mother remained local until the new baby was born. We began the process of selecting names for the unborn child. Tonya would research and write lists of names on sheets of paper in between caring for Spencer and Zach, which was a handful with the sudden presence of a toddler in the house. Everything had to be put away or upgraded for his safety: electrical plug guards, drawer stoppers, stairway gates, and on and on. Zach was into everything, and it was a leap into absolute free fall on Tonya's part.

The name that eventually stayed at the top of the list was Aiden. It was certainly my favorite. It is a Celtic name that means "little fire." It was perfect to me, not only because of the time I had spent in Scotland as a young man, but because I had a dream, much like the dreams Tonya had been having during this crazy time of adoption and rebuilding a family.

In my dream, I was in a wheat field similar to the ones where I grew up. The sky was that violet color it became right at dusk, just before the sun fell behind the horizon. I stood quietly in the field, running my fingertips over the top of the soft, prickly beards of wheat. As I did so, I felt a hush come across the entire field, then saw two figures coming toward me: a woman and a child.

As they came closer, I recognized the woman as Tamara and the child as an older version of Griffin. He was now running and playing at the feet of his mother. He appeared to be about four-years-old—the age he would have been in this life had we not lost him in the accident. He hid shyly behind his mother as she came to a stop in front of me. He clung to her white cotton skirt and peaked around her legs in a teasing manner.

She smiled at me and said, "I wanted to show you something." She reached around and gently pulled him in front of her. Cupping his face under his chin, he smiled knowingly at me. I knew it was Griffin; I felt his soul and our connection. He was beautiful. As I looked at him deeply, feeling our spirits connect yet again, I actually saw the look of Zach in his eyes. His eyes were always that striking crystal blue, but it was only in this moment that I realized he and Zach had the same eyes, strong eyes.

I felt the connection I was developing with Zach. I knew, even though he was adopted, that he was much like me. I let all those feelings sink in, and as they did, another vision flashed before me in the dream. It was a quick little image, like a subliminal frame in a movie, but I saw it clearly. There was another little boy with radiant, almost orange, strawberry-blond hair, and although it was a quick glimpse, I knew this was the unborn child that was soon coming. I looked at Tamara, and she only smiled, acknowledging that I got the message.

As I awoke, I felt a deep love for Tonya and all she was doing and bringing into my life, even if it was frightening and on a fast track. I thought about what I had seen in the dream and the little boy with fire-colored hair. I knew his name would be Aiden, "little fire." It was perfect.

Several weeks after that dream, the adoption agency called and

explained that the delivery date was approaching and that the birth mother had requested Tonya to be with her during the birth.

Tonya was a little apprehensive, but I convinced her it would be a beautiful experience, so we agreed. A few days later the social worker called us they were driving to the hospital. Our birth mother was now in labor, and Aiden was on his way! At that point, our birth mother requested that I too join them in the birthing room. Now I also felt Tonya's apprehension. I was different since I was a man, but this time Tonya convinced me that we should both be there.

As the labor progressed, Tonya had joined the birth mother at her bedside and was holding her hand and feeding her ice chips. I, however, had found a seat at a comfortable distance away on the couch that was near the window of the birthing suite. As the labor became even more intense and progressive, the birth mother called for me to join them. I was confused and reluctant.

She saw my hesitation and yelled in that guttural, labor intense voice, "Are you the father of this child or not?"

"Yes, well no, but *yes*!" I replied.

"Then get over here!" she insisted.

I joined her and Tonya as Aiden came into the world. It was amazing. In fact, the doctor actually put me in gloves at the request of both Tonya and the birth mother, and I got to catch Aiden, cut his umbilical cord, and be the first to welcome him into this world. I gave him his first little bath and then passed him on to his mothers. It was a beautiful experience. I had witnessed him coming into the world just like I had my natural sons. And though Griffin was gone, I felt him smiling on the situation from above, knowing Spencer would now have not only one but two brothers.

I walked for a while outside, breathing in the evening air. Life was moving so fast, but it felt like blessings were flowing my way. I had a grateful spirit as I looked at the stars. I returned to get another look at Aiden. He was there in a blanket, dry from his bath and content. Sure enough, his hair had a definite orange tinge, and one look in his newborn eyes let me know he was the one I had seen in my dream. We brought him home. Tonya and I and our three boys set out to create a family.

CHAPTER 31

ONE INTERESTING FACT ABOUT our three boys was they all had something in common: each had a birth mother who was elsewhere. It was something that could later bond them, but I won't lie—it was mayhem. With one child we focused, with two we divided and conquered, but with three, all hell broke loose, and we simply held on tight and tried not to get bucked off.

With all the focus on marriage, family, and adoption, I had let things at the office slip. Our business was struggling, and my personal savings had been gobbled up in the adoption fees. We were going through layoffs and intense pressures at work, which caused me financial concern. Tonya was frazzled at home juggling three kids that had all come into her life at once. Between the stress at work, the sleep deprivation at home, and still actually working on my new marriage, I was barely holding it all together. I kept putting on a confident demeanor as if all was well, but it was a rugged adjustment. It truly was like drinking from a fire hose.

The next few years were a blur. It was like a crazy dream with so many complicated parts and details that it simply became mush. I had received many spiritual promptings along the way and followed them. I expected things to fall into place when I did so, yet it all felt like such chaos. I was doing what I thought was right. Why wasn't it easy? Why wasn't life smoother? Why all the challenges and setbacks? I was falling into an abyss of self-doubt. My only answers were to work harder, pray harder, and love more. I did all the things I thought would help, only to find I was still drowning in unmet expectations.

Tonya was not only dealing with the reality of jumping from single to married with three children in a whirlwind timeframe, but she also shouldered the culture shock of moving into a tight-knit Mormon community. It was smothering her.

Our boys were all displaying issues as well. Spencer became more introverted. Tonya was concerned enough to have him evaluated. I was in denial, telling myself he was just depressed and working through all the adjustments in his life, but Tonya knew there was more to it. She wanted to have him tested to make sure he was alright.

When we took him to a specialist, we learned what I had viewed as an interesting personality was actually diagnosed as Asperger's syndrome, a high-functioning form of autism. Zach was suffering from attachment disorder and displayed such horrible temper tantrums and fits that we sought assistance from the Children's Center at the university, a special every-day program for preschoolers with behavior issues. The level of his emotional and even physical distress was consistently so intense that we were concerned for his well-being.

Aiden was a demanding baby and displayed signs of what was eventually diagnosed as severe ADHD. We weren't just raising three boys, but taking on the challenges that came with special children, each of which had unique characteristics. The dynamic of all three together compounded our stress and caused much worry and restlessness. The demands at work continued to be stressful as well—managing demanding clients, deadlines, and working to maintain the financial obligations of a small company during the severe economic downturn resulting from the 9/11 attacks in New York, were all eating away at my contentment.

I found myself sometimes asking those "why" questions again: why this? Why now? I had been through so much and had gained a great deal of spiritual insights, but I was obviously still learning. Returning home on a regular basis after horrific days at work to find Tonya broken down, crying in bed, with the boys creating an emotional three-ring circus was depressing. I felt guilty, as if I had somehow talked Tonya into marrying me and made her miserable.

Granted, it was all her choice, but I felt responsible for her happiness, and she wasn't happy. I would imagine perhaps I should have just stayed single and raised Spencer on my own. Then the guilt of the car crash returned, and I felt as if I had ruined his life in some way as well. I looked at my two adopted little boys and felt there must be thousands of better fathers out there.

I even struggled as a man. My physical pain was constant, and though I worked through it day after day to provide a living, I felt as if Tonya deserved a whole man, not a crippled one with all the injuries and pain I dealt with. And what of my heart? It was still broken, too. I knew deep down I was still grieving, but I didn't dare talk about it with anyone. I was afraid to share my sorrow and my struggles.

I had moved on, right? I had remarried and adopted two beautiful babies. What was there to grieve? Why could I not just be grateful? But the emotional pain hadn't gone away. I even felt guilty about that. Why couldn't I quit hurting inside and just let it go? Despite this internal struggle, I kept it hidden from everyone. I carried false expectations about how to find its remedy. I expected Tonya and the boys to fix it. I even expected my career to fix it. I looked for anyone to simply validate me and make me feel better about myself.

I continually tried so hard to make everything work, yet my children were having issues, Tonya was struggling with her new life, and I grasped for what I knew was true. I tried to find what I had experienced spiritually, but it didn't manifest itself in the way I thought it would.

Tonya and I decided to sell the house and make a fresh start. We wanted to reset everything somewhere as simply "the Olsens," not the widower and his son, the new bride, and two adopted kids. It was tough to create unity with so many onlookers waiting and wondering what would become of the puzzle pieces of our lives.

The house sold relatively quickly, but we priced it to sell in a buyer's market, which didn't vastly improve our finances. We found a "fixer-upper" rambler across the street from the junior high school Spencer would soon be attending. We poured all our energy into the little house and made a beautiful home out of it. It was good to start fresh in a new neighborhood with unfamiliar surroundings and new people.

After a year or so in the new house, things at work began to improve. The boys were all doing better as well. Spencer mainstreamed into seventh grade, Zach transitioned out of the Children's Center, and under the direction of physicians, we were managing Aiden's ADHD relatively well.

Tonya and I still had work to do, however; somewhere in the middle of bawling kids, messy diapers, and the constant stress, I had lost her and myself. I had lost the magic of our relationship and how we came together.

I was still looking for external validation from the outside in, rather than from the inside out. I felt disjointed in many ways. I still had so many pieces to put back together within myself. I was constantly, secretly searching for comfort and validation. I wanted to feel that I was okay, that we were okay, and that I had made the right decisions. There was a massive, hollow void in my heart that could not be filled by anyone. Although I rebuilt a family, I had not rebuilt myself. I was only finding ways to dress the wound and would have to go much deeper to find true healing.

CHAPTER 32

I KNEW THE BEST WAY to get over feeling sorry for myself was to serve others. At the time of the accident, I saw people with no judgment, only unconditional love. I knew them at such a deep level and experienced the oneness and connection we all share. I wanted to feel that way again. I wanted to see others as God saw them, and see myself as God saw me. I decided to recreate my experience in some way, if I could, and the cherry tree in the backyard of our rambler house was the perfect opportunity.

Spencer and I went out and picked several five-gallon buckets of fresh cherries from the large tree in our backyard. We washed them and bagged them into quart-sized Ziploc bags. I knew that even if we froze most of them we would never be able to eat them all, so we created a game out of the situation. We decided to sit down and listen to our hearts so we'd be guided as to who might be most deserving of the fresh cherries.

As I sat quietly, a simple verse came into my heart: "I was a stranger and ye took me in." Then the prompting hit me: what if we actually took the cherries to strangers instead of friends and neighbors? We'd close our eyes and just practice feeling inspiration as to where to go with the cherries, and then who to give them to. Spencer and I drove around, giving the cherries to random folks along the way. They laughed and were grateful. Some were a bit apprehensive, but most were taken aback and warmed by the randomness and the kindness. We eventually ended up near my office in downtown Salt Lake City, still armed with several bags of cherries.

At one point, we were driving along the west side of Pioneer Park when Spencer asked me to stop. I pulled the truck off to the side of the road. He closed his eyes for a while, and then he opened them and told me he got the message. He got out of the truck and headed toward a rough-looking homeless man sitting in the park. Needless to say, I was apprehensive as a father, but I kept a close eye on Spencer as he approached the man and held out the cherries. I watched them exchange in a brief conversation. The man took the cherries and held the Ziploc bag as if it was sacred as they talked some more. The man eventually buried his head in his hands and started quivering with sobbing gestures as Spencer ran back toward the truck.

I asked him what had happened. He told me the man reminisced about his home and his mother. The man told him they had a big cherry tree in their yard when he was a little boy and that the cherries reminded him of his mom. This was a big lesson for both of us, and something I really needed. I wanted to give myself a break from the day-to-day and get back in touch with spiritual things, remembering my connection to the divine. By putting all judgments aside and simply following our hearts, my son and I created miracles that day.

Something as simple as a Ziploc bag of cherries became a cherished gift and memory, a link from a broken life to a loving past. It was also a vivid reminder that we are all connected. I realized I had all my own answers within myself if I chose to seek them. By simply being still and listening to that little voice that spoke to the heart and then trusting it, we had known exactly where to be, whom to speak to, and what to say in every moment.

I wanted every day to be like that. I wanted to do that in my home life, too. It was one thing to go out and engage with strangers for an afternoon, but what about those times at home when it was difficult and challenges came up? Would I implement my heart and know what to say and how to handle every situation? I still struggled greatly with my inner wounds. Spreading healing to others was good, and watching Spencer enjoy the bliss of doing that was even better, but I still wasn't connecting the experience to my own painful past and personal healing. I wanted someone to bring me the fresh cherries, the fruit that would give me a brighter outlook on life and true, inner healing.

My mistake was expecting someone else to deliver the fruit to me. My pain was in counting on others to fill my inner void. I wanted to feel that same love we created that afternoon, but I was forgetting the only one who could create it for me was *me*. I was so busy battling to put all of my personal puzzle pieces back together that I was missing the big picture of what I was really trying to create. If I wanted to experience the same love, peace, and joy, then I had to embrace it from within myself. How could I expect to give what I did not have, and how was I to find it with the huge hole still in my heart?

I worried about my boys. Would I ever be the father they deserved? I worried about Tonya. Would I ever be the husband she dreamed of? Although I created brief moments of light through community service, connecting with my sons, and spending quiet time alone, I felt I was slipping into darkness. Nothing I did on the outside would bring enough light to heal me from the inside. I was drowning in self-loathing and insecurities about everything—about me being enough for Tonya and the boys, my ability to provide for them, my capacity to juggle work and civil activities that seemed to be multiplying daily. I even began to doubt my connection to God and to my angels. I was going through the motions, sleepwalking, but forgetting who I really was and my connection to light.

CHAPTER 33

THE MONTHS AND YEARS rolled on, and our boys each grew joyfully in personality, but each had their challenges. Spencer became very interested in music. He was playing bass guitar in several bands and was becoming a talented musician. It was a wonderful way for him to express himself nonverbally, since verbal communication was sometimes difficult for him. As adolescence came, the sweet, shy, supportive child had become an angry young man. Spencer struggled at times in his relationship with Tonya. He struggled to fit in socially as well. At least music provided him with a like-minded peer group through high school, but I wondered about the influences he was attracting to himself. He was into pretty heavy, dark music and had become more and more reclusive.

Zach became our athletic child, excelling in sports but struggling to find his place. Even though he was good at everything he did, he didn't enjoy sports and felt I was forcing him to participate in them. I wasn't. I enjoyed watching and coaching him, but to him it felt simply like pressure to compete and excel. I feared he only saw my enthusiasm as an unreachable expectation of some kind. He was resentful and tried to distance himself from me. By early adolescence Zach found passion in musical theater, dance, and drama. I was enthusiastic and supportive of that as well, but knew too little about it to connect with him beyond watching. Perhaps that was good; maybe it took all the pressure off.

Aiden was the family comedian. His sense of humor and wit were beyond his years, but they were often inappropriate. Maybe that's why it seemed so funny. Humor was his coping mechanism to fit in. He was closely connected with Spencer but was growing up way too fast, trying to fit in with his older brother and his high school friends. Aiden truly was funny, and kept us all laughing with his silly impressions and antics. I suppose laughter was good between the tears.

With the boys' difficulties came my own. Tonya and I had become disconnected. We had given everything to our children, to maintaining the house, and to my career, and yet so little energy now went to each other. We didn't talk, touch, or really connect to each other at all. We had lost our intimacy, not just physically, but emotionally as well. That candle we left burning on that little table on my country bridge years ago was barely flickering. The constant storm had diminished it to only a glowing wick.

As Spencer graduated and left for college, a piece of me left with him. I realized that so much of my energy had been wrapped up in him making up for the guilt I felt over the crash. The hole in my heart seemed to expand even larger when he moved out. The emptiness he had been filling was now void, too. Reality hit me right in the face: had I done enough to raise him strong? Was he aware enough to be a man and make good decisions? Had my secret self-doubt and insecurities translated to him vicariously in any way? It was too late to correct any of that now. He was leaving and might never live under our roof again. The plain truth was that time had run out, and all I could do had already been done, yet it had blown by in a blur.

As Spencer left, I thought about when I left for college. I pondered what drove me during those volatile years when I was not a man but thought I knew everything about life. And yet at that point, what life had taught me was that things didn't always work out. People were hard to trust. The feeling that I was not good enough, and a desire to prove to everyone somehow that I was, had been my biggest motivator.

It seemed like a sickness as I looked back on it, yet there I was still living the same way: feeling so small, striving for all kinds of accolades and recognition, not only at work but also from Tonya and anyone else who would throw them my way. It was all a bandage for my own feelings of inadequacy in spite of all I had experienced. And no one knew—no one but me. It was my big secret. Even with all the incredible things that had happened to me, I still needed others to tell me I was okay. I wondered where all those insecurities came from. Where did this all start? Why did I have such an inferiority complex?

I actually broke down at the office working late one night after everyone had gone. I cried out to God, and for the first time in many years it was sincere. "Why, God?" I demanded aloud. "What's wrong with me? Why do I feel this way? Why is there never enough?"

There was silence. I heard and felt nothing, which left me even emptier and still searching. I wondered if I could only draw from my earlier answers at the time of the accident, but now it seemed so long ago. I could not deny what I had felt, seen, and experienced then, but where were those answers now? I felt so alone. Why has God forgotten me? Had I messed up my life beyond His reach? In my quest to truly become nonjudgmental, had I lost all good judgment? There had been so many choices that didn't work, so much heartache and let-downs. I had disappointed so many people in so many ways, mostly my family, and for sure, myself. Letting myself down was the most painful.

In the spring of 2009, I finally came to Tonya in a broken heap and poured out all my shame and pain. Confessing my deepest regrets, I shared with her all the parts of my life that didn't work. I explained everything I'd done in my attempt to cover up my pain and loneliness. I expected her to turn me away and realize that I was different than the strong mask I had always put on for her. However, through it all, she simply showed me love and acceptance. Everything I had hidden from her in fear of her seeing me as bad, weak, small, or inadequate, she forgave. She freely absolved me of everything that I had been holding against myself for so long. It was a miracle.

My mind rushed back in time to when I first met Tonya and how I fell in love with her. I recalled the promptings I was given from the beginning of our relationship, including the experience I had at Tamara's grave. All these years through the struggles I thought I was learning to love her unconditionally, when in reality I was actually being taught by her unconditional love for me. It was I who didn't love myself. Tamara had been right on; Tonya taught me unconditional love by putting me in situations where I would finally learn to fully love myself.

It was such a powerful and profound experience. That little candle we had started burning on the stormy night of our engagement so long ago now burned brightly again. The wind and rain only made it stronger and more determined to radiate light into our darkness, and that light changed everything. I acknowledged, however, that the only thing that had changed was me; the situations remained the same. The boys and their challenges, my work and its demands, our relationship and the intricacies of piecing a family back together, it was all still there. My perspective, however, had changed, and that was the miracle.

Peace had finally come. All these years I had beat myself up over so many things. I had doubted my choices and blamed myself when things didn't go splendidly. I had spent so many sleepless nights lying awake, wondering and listening to the voices in my head. I spent so many hours at work avoiding what was happening at home. But now, peace and light were here. I finally rested in a way that I hadn't in so long. I did often wish I could go back and start all over again. I wanted to reverse time and do things differently with what I knew now. Tonya deserved this newer, whole me from the beginning of our relationship.

I drifted into sleep one night not long after all this with the notion that I really wanted a completely fresh start with Tonya without all we had been through. As I slept, Tamara actually came to me in another dream. She ran up and put her arms around my neck. She swung around me, dancing joyfully, and kissed me on my face. Then she stopped twirling and looked me right in the eyes.

She spoke but only said this simple phrase: "All that exists here is wisdom."

That's all she said aloud, but she continued to look at me and communicate without words. A flood of knowledge flowed between us. She communicated that it didn't matter what I had done or what I didn't do. All that mattered was what I had learned from it. All that existed in the heavenly realms was wisdom. My burdens could be made light, not as in less heavy, but actually by being illuminated into light. My choices, and the results of those choices, were only there for me to learn from, and those lessons simply brought about wisdom.

It had all been a blessing. There was no reason to go back or to feel deep regret for the things I could not change. We had created the experience together and now stood on higher ground. We could start fresh from right there and move forward without having to erase what in reality had brought us wisdom.

I awoke with a fresh, new heart. The hole in me seemed much smaller now. Tonya hadn't filled it. Even Tamara and the dream had not filled it, but *I* was finally filling it by validating myself. The light was within me and always had been. I had just turned it off and forgotten.

CHAPTER 34

THE DREAM HAD BEEN good to ground me, but there was still so much to work through. I continued to suffer from feelings of insecurity at times that caused arguments between Tonya and I. I found myself in my office late one night after one such argument, again asking God where all my insecurities had come from. However, this time, I questioned Him in a much different spirit.

I wasn't angrily demanding answers, but trusting, and knowing God was there for me. I had laid down on my office floor to stretch my back out. It was late enough that no one was around, however, I still reached over to swing my office door shut for privacy. As I lay there contemplating all the drama I seemed to be causing in my own life, I began to pray aloud.

"Why, God? When did this all start?" I asked. "Why have I lived a life of feeling so inadequate, even though I am enough? Where did all the insecurities come from?"

As smoothly as I asked, the answers flowed into my understanding. I actually saw myself vividly in my mind's eye: I was four years old behind the couch in my childhood home. My mom and dad were splitting up, and I didn't know why. I watched as the little boy's heart broke. I saw him, me, heaving with sobs and emotions, this perfect little boy, innocent, breaking as his world crumbled before him.

I looked at my four-year-old self. I recognized those little boy hands, those hand-me-down jeans, and that hair, how Mom had trimmed it over the ears and across the forehead with her sewing scissors on the back porch of the house. I looked on, feeling his pain but from my current adult perspective. I was compelled to go to him, so I did.

It was as real and vivid as if I was really doing it. I bent down by that smaller, earlier version of myself, and I picked him up and comforted him. I felt his little hands on my neck as I wiped his tears and we made eye contact. I assured him that he was okay, that everything would turn out alright. He smiled, and I remembered that crooked little-boy smile. I was hugging me!

"It all turns out, you know," I said to my little self. "We are only here to learn. All that exists is wisdom."

And love, I thought as the much younger, much smaller me leaned into my chest and stopped crying. All these years I had carried all that pain and insecurity, but now it was gone. The key was that the healing had always been up to me. I had had the answers all along.

As quickly as life had seemed to spiral out of control, it was now ascending into something new. It felt so different to be with Tonya now. We fell in love all over again. It didn't take big things. We now simply made time for each other and really looked at each other. We connected, listened, and touched. We even played Yahtzee from time-to-time. I was healing from within. I was offering her a whole man, no matter what body parts were missing.

All these years, I had expected Tonya to meet me in the middle. I had thought that if I gave fifty percent, she would give fifty, and we would somehow create a whole. But now I was whole on my own. I no longer needed her validation, nor anyone else's. I had my own power, my own light. I was bringing one hundred percent to the table. Now, I simply chose her. There was no need or expectations, only love, which I could give freely because I was finally beginning to love myself.

My focus returned to my boys and how I could show up for them in more powerful ways. Spencer had been struggling at school to find his faith and answers. His grades were high but his emotions low, and he was wading through his own darkness. Zach was experiencing sadness over being adopted and had been searching for his own identity in many ways. Aiden was having a difficult time focusing enough in school to learn what was expected and was falling behind.

I looked forward to the summer months and a break from all of it simply to reconnect with Tonya and the boys. We planned a weekend trip to the family cabin for fishing on the lake, hiking in the hills, and unplugging from the world for a while.

The weather was beautiful, and we enjoyed being with family and in nature. Tonya relaxed in the sun by the lake with her sisters-in-law while I fished with Aiden. Zach and his cousins all went swimming and played in the shallow end of the water. Spencer took a four-wheeler on one of the small mountain trails to explore and clear his head.

Everyone was doing what he or she loved while resting and interacting with extended family. It felt like heaven was right here on earth—the smell of fresh trees and the lake in the air sprinkled by the laughter of dear ones, the random hawk in flight or elk wandering into the meadow. For the first time in a long time, I felt peace. My heart was finally right, and that rippled out into everything around me.

CHAPTER 35

O N THE EVENING OF our second day, we gathered in the cabin around a roaring fire for dinner. My younger brother, Justin, grilled the catch of the day out on the deck while the rest of us set the table and debated which card games to play after dinner. The only one missing was Spencer.

As it became darker, I began to worry about where he might be. He had been out on the four-wheeler all day. I was sure he knew his way back but wondered, as it got dark, why he hadn't returned. I was concerned that something had happened or if he had run out of gas. The cell service was poor in the mountains, and he would have no way of reaching us if something had gone wrong.

We were just about to go out looking for him when he pulled up. He was quiet and looked concerned.

"I want to talk to you, Dad," he said sternly as he parked the four-wheeler and entered the cabin.

"Come in, Son. Sit down," I replied.

"No, Dad, I want to talk to you in private."

I walked out onto the porch and asked what was going on.

"Can we go for a ride or something away from everyone?" he answered.

It was already dark and getting cold, so I grabbed the truck keys and beckoned him to climb in. We drove down the trail and onto the main road in silence.

"What's up, Son?" I asked apprehensively, not sure that I actually wanted to hear the answer.

"I don't know. I just need to talk."

"What's on your mind?"

Spencer sat silently, looking out the window into the darkness. My heartbeat quickened as I wondered what he might say. He was hard to read. At least he was willing to talk to me, if he would.

He sat still, just gazing out the window. I pulled the truck off the dirt lane and sat, waiting for him to speak. "I don't know what to think, Dad," he started in soft, unsure tones. "I don't know if I believe you."

I swallowed hard. "How so, Son? I've never lied to you."

"You speak of a God who loves us," Spencer continued. "You speak of these profound experiences and dreams you've had. You talk about healing and answers. I don't get any of that!"

I sat in silence, not knowing what to say, and watched as he became more emotional.

"You speak of having peeked into heaven, and leaving your body after the crash. You got to say good-bye to Mom and Griffin. You told me how they come to you in dreams and visions. I've never had any of that. In fact, that's where I was today: I went out on the four-wheeler to find a secluded place. I knew that here, in this peaceful place, I could get an answer. I poured my heart out all day. I begged God for a feeling or anything, but nothing came. I wanted proof or some kind of sign."

As I listened, I felt my own eyes moisten as tears began to roll down his cheeks.

"There was nothing, Dad. Nothing! For twelve years, I have begged God to just let me see Mom, even once. For twelve years, I begged God to allow me to feel something. Anything! But there has been nothing. And today again, I went in full faith. I knew if God was there, He would give me an answer, but nothing came. Just emptiness. So, either you're deceived in some way, or if God is there, he certainly doesn't care about me!"

He fell over against the window and started to cry, my six-foot-two young man breaking down. I sat watching. All I could do was put my hand on his shoulder. He sat up and wiped his eyes and nose with his hand. He looked right at me.

"I'm done with it, Dad," Spencer told me. "I'm done with believing. I've lost my faith. I want nothing to do with religion or any of it. I've begged almost every day for years and never have I experienced anything. You've had all these beautiful experiences. You've seen all these things, but for me, it's been nothing like that."

His face fell back into his hands. My tears now flowed too as I felt the intensity of his pain. I didn't know what to say. He leaned back against the window again, and I put my hand back on his shoulder.

I knew he wasn't mad at me; he was mad at God and was telling me about it openly and honestly. I wasn't mad at him, either. This was the little boy who had been so supportive. He had loved me so much. When I came home so physically and spiritually broken after nearly five months in the hospital, he told me he would love me, "Even if I was nothing but a puddle of blood."

Now he was questioning me and doubting my experiences And I still didn't know what to say. I had shared everything with Spencer, but knowing he had petitioned for so long, for anything, with no answer, hurt me almost as deeply as it did him.

Spencer gained his composure as we sat in the darkness. There was nothing to say. I'd forfeit all my experiences for him to have some kind of "knowing" of his own. I wondered why some people have spiritual things happen and others didn't. It obviously has nothing to do with our willingness or being deserving. Why me and not my innocent child?

I thought of all those nights when Spencer went to his room as a little boy, and unbeknownst to me, begged God to send him any kind of comfort. I thought of those dark nights in his adolescence when he was so open but the door to heaven remained shut. I wondered about nights like this in his early adult life when even in his faith and willingness, nothing came in spite of his cries. Why did God provide experiences for some and not for others?

I had no answer for him. Even as his mortal father, I had no comfort to give beyond just sitting there, hurting with him. It wasn't fair. What about life ever was? I blessed him in the only way I knew how to as a father. When we had both gained our composure, I mustered up the only words that came to mind:

"Sometimes when we seek signs, the signs never come," I said. "And there may never be a burning bush or thunder and lightning from the sky, but I know what I experienced was real. And I also know your answers will come to you at some point. It will be in a special way and at a special time, and probably when you least expect it, but it will be just for you. It may be a simple hushed whisper in your heart or a gentle, subtle feeling in the air, but I know Mom and Griff will let you know they're there. And in knowing they're there, you'll know God is there too, and that He loves you."

Spencer looked at me, unsure.

"Okay, I'll make you a deal," I said. "If and when I die, I will come to you. I will come to you in some way that you will know it's me and it will be undeniable. Okay?"

That's all I could say. There would never be any proof, but I wanted Spencer to find his own light; I didn't want him living on my faith and my experiences. It went far beyond him finding religion. I wanted him to find peace, and simply be happy.

CHAPTER 36

O N SUNDAY AFTERNOON, WE all went our separate ways. Spencer headed north to Logan, and Tonya and I went home with the younger boys.

I did a lot of soul-searching after our conversation. This began quite a journey for me, everything from studying spiritual modalities like Reiki and spending time with Native American shamans, to doing intense experiential training. I delved much deeper into my own faith and embraced its symbols on a much higher level. I really began praying again, trusting and listening. I read and reread a lot of good books—all of which served me well.

I asked God to touch Spencer in some way that he could comprehend. I called upon our deceased loved ones to come to him. I now begged for my son to receive assistance from heaven in some kind of meaningful way, like I had. And if Spencer didn't want religion, perhaps he could obtain spirituality and direction in his own quiet way, which felt even more important to me than anything else.

After our trip, I began to have more vivid dreams, and more often. One night before bed, I was contemplating Spencer's path and found that I was actually on a renewed path of my own. I pondered on the notion of religion versus spirituality and how it all fit. I was beginning to see a strong thread of truth that ran throughout so many aspects of my own life and came from many diverse sources. My last conscious thought was that the role of any religion was to assist one in reaching personal spirituality. However, no matter the religion, powerful personal spirituality was the desired end goal.

As I slept, I had a vivid dream where I was shown three people. I was first shown Gandhi, whom I knew little about except for the few things I had learned in history classes. I was shown his life: how he lived, what he did, and how he loved. I witnessed his religion, Hinduism, and what it meant to him and how he embraced the traditions and symbols of his personal culture and beliefs. It was inspiring. He was wonderful.

I was then shown a woman, Mother Teresa of Calcutta, a Catholic nun. I was shown her life: how she lived and how she loved. I witnessed her religion and what it meant to her—her traditions and symbols and the beauty she found within them.

Then I saw Jesus, yet I was shown him as a Jewish man practicing his Jewish ceremonies and symbols throughout his life, right up until the end. I was shown how he lived: what he did, how he loved, and what he stood for. I witnessed his religion and what it meant to him personally. The power he found in the traditions and symbols of his culture was beautiful.

As the vision of these three astounding individuals came to an end, a voice in the dream said this to me: "It was not their religion that gave them power. Their power came from knowing who they were and their connection to the Creator." I realized that in that knowledge, they lived and loved in divine ways, and so could I.

These three distinctive people from diverse cultures and theologies were unified in the way they loved and their knowledge of their divine connection to our divine source.

After that, I embraced my own religion in much different, yet more meaningful ways than I had previously. I now saw the deeper beauty in my own symbols and ceremonies. Yet, in the same breath, truth and spirituality were now far more important to me than religion.

I began to see profound, symbolic meaning in many diverse religious ordinances that I hadn't before. I also saw that they were simply symbolic of something much greater. I remembered I had been shown this at the time of the accident in a profound way, but now it was finally beginning to click. I knew I could fully embrace my culture and my traditions, but my spiritual power was only found in a very personal connection with and direct communication from God.

I wanted Spencer and our entire family to find that same truth. My experiences over the years had transformed my hope and faith into absolute trust. I knew that whatever my circumstances, they were perfect for my soul's progression. I trusted the process, which I knew was customized and designed perfectly for me individually. And if my experience here was in such good hands, then I knew all those around me were in those same good hands. Even my children. *Especially* my children.

For so long I had hovered over them as a father, protecting them, making their decisions, and seeing that they did what I thought they were supposed to do. My motivation was love, and I simply wanted them to be happy and successful but that was quickly shifting. I was now able to respect and honor them as eternal beings that were capable of making their own decisions and then learning from the consequences of their choices. After all, isn't that what God does with all of us? He grants us free will and choice, then lovingly allows us to learn and grow from the experience of our choices. We thereby are accountable in the end for what we have created and how we have grown. There is no finger-pointing, blame, or judgment.

By letting go of my judgment, I actually saw my children in their magnificence as young men, while no longer holding them in smallness as helpless little ones. They were not helpless, nor have they ever been. They were strong and noble souls, simply going through the process of defining who they were.

I also embraced experience as the only true teacher. I thought of my own adolescence and early adulthood, recalling all those long chalkboard talks in the high school and college football locker rooms. In theory, every play was a touchdown, or stopped at the line of scrimmage, depending on your perspective of offense or defense. I remembered watching all those game films and theorizing about how it was done and what would work.

But in truth, I had no idea how fast a four-point-four-second forty was until I was actually on the field, experiencing it. That was the only way to really grow. I got knocked around a lot and missed some tackles, but boy did I learn from having the actual experience. Otherwise, how would I know? Sure, I made a few plays as well, and that felt good, but the more intense learning sometimes came from really messing up. Life was like that. It's our greatest teacher. The things we experience here and the truths we take to heart from those experiences are all that really matter. They are the wisdom we get to keep.

I began to trust that Spencer would find his way, as would all of us, but it would look completely different than my way, or Tonya's, his brothers', or anyone else's in this world. And that was okay; in fact, it finally made perfect sense.

CHAPTER 37

As I pondered these profound truths, my mind wandered back to Spencer, his faith, and his individuality. He dove into a process of literally manifesting who and what he chose to be. He too was soul-searching, reading a lot, pondering, doing intense trainings, and was being very open to whatever he might learn. He looked into diverse ideas and then felt what was true for him. He was simply walking his path, so I decided to walk with him, from a distance, without hovering, judging, or feeling like I had to save him.

Eventually everything shifted in a dramatic fashion. It was not without hard work, but Spencer did find his own powerful answers. By the end of that summer, he came to me again, this time not in private. Tonya was with me. He was every bit as sober as the first time and with even more tears, but now he came with tears of joy. He gave me a big bear hug and just held on.

While still embracing me, he said, "I love you, Dad, and I believe you. It's all real. Mom's there, and it's all okay. I know what I know now, and nobody can ever take that away."

I pulled back to look at him. All I saw was pure joy. I saw that happy little boy Spencer had been before the crash, but now in a young man's body. His eyes were filled with light, and his smile was illuminated. I didn't have to ask what had happened; somehow, I already knew. He then turned to

Tonya and actually cupped her face in his hands. He looked her right in the eye, which he hadn't done for so long.

"I love you," he said. "Thank you for everything you have done for me. For coming to us and being my mom."

That uncorked my emotions, and my own tears flowed freely. We all stood there, clinging to each other, and wept for joy. The most beautiful part was it had nothing to do with me. My son had experienced his own miracle, and he created it for himself. It was the most satisfying thing as a father to know that he didn't need me. He had become a man, on his own, with all his own answers.

I believed the wish of every father was to see his children grow up better than he was, that they could stand on their own two feet and be independently strong. I didn't realize until that moment that I was inadvertently raising my sons to never need me again, but that was actually the end goal. And that's exactly what I witnessed in this sacred moment.

I watched Spencer continue to mature during the next year. We spent time together, studied together, trained together, and talked a lot. On one occasion, one of Spencer's friends had gone to jail on drug charges. He had a court hearing of some kind, and Spencer announced that he would be attending the hearing in support of his friend.

In my judgment I said, "You will not! You're not going to be associated with known drug dealers."

Spencer looked at me in surprise. "Is that how it is, Dad?" he asked. "When somebody messes up, we turn our backs on them and ignore them? I'm going to stand with my friend. I may be the only one there to say, 'It's okay, I'm here for you and we'll get through this.'"

I knew Spencer was right. I was actually proud of him for standing up to me. I realized then that he had always been a teacher to me; from the time he was born until now, he had come as a mentor, a leader, and a light to my own path. Even when I felt he was lost and going through darkness, it had actually served as a backward way of showing me the light. I wondered if his spirit was wiser and older than mine and I was just catching up. There seemed to be such cosmic order to all that was happening and had happened.

My heart expanded to my other sons. I looked forward to what they would create in their lives. My thoughts turned to my little son, Griffin. I wondered what part he must be playing in all of this. I longed for him. Each time my thoughts turned to him, I wondered what might have been—and what perhaps, in reality, was—based on knowing he was there somehow, involved in it all from another realm.

I dreamt of Griffin that night. It was one of those strange, lucid dreams where I couldn't truthfully say whether I was asleep or awake. I sat on the front seat of my dad's old white pickup truck. I remembered that truck in every detail. As I looked down, I realized I wore a toddler's jumpsuit, the kind that had the snaps all along the inner legs for easy diaper access. It was red corduroy. I followed the material down my legs to see that I was wearing little white lace-up shoes.

I remembered this! I never liked that jumpsuit nor the shoes. I remember being here, being small, and wearing this. I looked out the window and noticed I was in the pasture at our Wallsburg ranch. The Black Angus beef cattle were all crowding against the truck to get at the feed in the truck bed.

I became frightened because in my toddler mind I thought the cattle might tip the truck over or get inside somehow. I felt uneasy when suddenly the cattle scattered and my dad jumped into the cab of the truck with me. He comforted me. It was like I was there, experiencing it all over again. I couldn't have been more than fourteen months old. Then it hit me: fourteen months old. That's the age Griffin was when I lost him in the crash, and here I was experiencing a moment from my own life when I was that same age.

Griffin! I thought as I looked out the truck window in my dream. As I did so, the truck, the cattle, and my dad all vanished, and I was suddenly my current age standing in the pasture. Immediately to the left of me was my son Griffin, except he was not a fourteen-month-old at all. He stood before me as a full-grown twenty-something-year-old man. It was like looking in the mirror: he was so like me in features and build, but taller and more muscular. He was magnificent.

I wanted to rush to him, but his gaze stopped me. He looked directly in my eyes, and the nonverbal communication that so often takes place in my dreams began. Without using words, he communicated to me: "I wanted you to see this so that you would know I will always remember having you as my dad."

I realized Griffin had taken me back to that moment in my life and allowed me to remember it with all the vivid details to make his point. I was literally experiencing that time is not *linear*, but *circular*. His brief life with me was as clear in eternity as those brief moments I had just re-experienced from my childhood. I comprehended with clarity that he was grateful for me being his father and he being my son, and also his pure intention of what he wanted me to experience in the dream.

His gaze softened, and I rushed to him. I threw my arms around Griffin and leaned my head into his strong jaw. We hugged tightly, heart-to-heart, for what felt like a few minutes. Then he did speak, his words went right into my ear. "I have a message for you, Dad," he said. My spirit leaped with joy: a message from heaven, from my son. I expected something profound and prophetic as I leaned into him to get the message.

"I love you, Dad. And I'm proud of you."

That was a far simpler and more powerful message than anything. I had struggled, loved, worked with, ached over, and had so much joy in my living sons, but I was now communing with the son I lost, who was now a grown, powerful, magnificent man. What a perfect gift.

I awoke with my eyes still wet. Was it real, and was "dream" even the appropriate word for such an experience? It didn't matter; it was real to me, and that was all that counted. To me, the dream showed that we are always connected, no matter what side of the veil we may be on. I learned that even the little things we did as parents mattered. The moments we create are eternal, and memories are sacred and important. I learned that, no matter what my shortcomings as a father might be, my love would always come through perfectly.

CHAPTER 38

I WAS SITTING IN A work meeting when my phone kept buzzing in my back pocket. I ignored it the first time, but when it began buzzing a second time just moments after, I decided I better see who it was. By the time I had discretely wedged it from my back pocket, I had missed the second call as well. There were two missed calls from Spencer. I knew it must be important. I excused myself from the meeting and immediately called him back.

Spencer was in college 110 miles away. If he called, he typically left a message, but two calls with no messages was odd. Spencer had recently moved off campus to a little rental house with a yard. He was an upper-class man now, and would be graduating the following spring.

I had some anxiety as his phone rang with no answer after four rings, then he finally picked up.

"Hey, Dad," Spencer began. "It's Sport." Because Spencer now had a yard, he recently rescued a puppy and named it Sport. "He's been hit by car, Dad. I don't know what to do"

"How bad is it?" I asked.

"It's pretty bad," he replied. "I mean, he is alive. His back leg is mangled. I'm not sure what else might be wrong. I gathered him up from the street and rushed him to the vet as fast as I could. They're going to check him out and let me know."

"Veterinarians can be expensive," I warned him. "How soon will they let you know?"

"I don't know."

I heard the apprehension in his voice, but I wanted to shoot straight with him. "You can't afford large expenses on top of school trying to save the dog, Son. If he's really bad, it might be most humane to put him down. I don't want to be harsh, but you must consider what his quality of life might be, and what extent you're willing to pursue to save him if his injuries are extensive."

"I don't know what happened," Spencer insisted. "I can't see how he got out!"

"There's no use worrying about that now," I tried to reassure him. "Let me know what they say about the dog and we'll have to make a decision."

"Ok, but I don't want to put him down."

"I know, but we may have no choice. Or it may still be best, depending on what we find out."

"Ok," Spencer conceded. "I will call you as soon as I know."

I hung up the phone and contemplated what my son might be going through. He'd had a lot of trauma in his young life, and this little accident with Sport might be tearing some things open for him. I wasn't sure, but he seemed pretty shaken up.

Spencer had also fallen in love that semester; that's why he had rescued the dog. He and his girlfriend, Ashley, had gone to the dog pound together and selected a puppy they both felt was special. I'm sure that added to the emotion of it all.

I remembered thinking at one time in my life that everything I loved always left me. From my early adolescent years to the accident, it seemed that when I got attached, something went wrong; my dad's second marriage ending, getting dumped by high school girlfriends, and then the accident and losing my own family.

I realized this was simply a puppy, but I didn't want Spencer to develop a similar pattern in losing the things he loved. He had a good head on his shoulders and I knew he would make the appropriate decision with or without my input. It was simply hard to watch my child hurt, even though he was a grown man. I silently sent some prayers his way for everyone involved, including the dog, and went back into my meeting until Spencer called me back.

The meeting was well over by the time I heard back from my oldest son.

"They're going to have to amputate Sport's leg, Dad," Spencer told me.

I knew the results of amputation far too well and how it affected my quality of life. Yet this was a puppy and I had no idea how it might affect a dog.

"Is that worth it, Son?" I asked. "How much will that cost and how active and happy can a three-legged dog be?"

"The vet says he'll have some healing to do, but that he should be alright if everything goes well."

"Ok, but how much is the surgery and what if it doesn't go well? Are you sure it's worth it? I mean, losing a leg is a big deal. I would know. What will his quality of life be?"

"That all remains to be seen, but we're going to do it." Spencer's voice was filled with clarity and conviction. "I know it's expensive, but we're going to do all we can at this point. Look at you, Dad: you do great missing a limb. No one would question your quality of life. I love you. I will call as soon as we know how things go."

Again, I was taught by my son's unwavering faith. He possessed an intense commitment to see things through and make best of any challenge, no matter the cost. Why give up hope on a dog, even if it lost a leg? No one had ever given up on me, no matter how awkwardly I walked. I still had much to offer and, as it turned out, Sport did, too. He was an extremely smart dog and was as active as ever, even on three legs. One hardly noticed, actually. He still had an uncanny way of escaping, too, but he knew full well to stay out of the street. Life did that to all of us; we learned, and our most powerful teacher was experience.

We laughed about how we had a three-legged dog and a one-legged man in the family. We must be quite a sight when we all get together. However, through it all, there are big lessons of trust and tenacity. And isn't that what life was all about: trust and tenacity? In other words, we did everything in our power with clear intention to resolve a situation, while trusting that the entire universe supported us.

If I applied that to every big and little situation, there was always an answer to the challenges that came our way. There was always light at the end of the tunnel. There was always a way to win and walk away (or limp, if I had to) with my head held high and my heart intact. And if I was lucky, I would walk away with new wisdom, increased trust, and magnified love.

CHAPTER 39

I WAS JUST WRAPPING UP a business lunch when my phone buzzed. This one was not a phone call, but a text message. I discreetly checked my phone to see who it was. It was from my little sister, wanting to know if I had time to talk. My younger sister was in the midst of a pregnancy, and she rarely texted or wanted to talk during the day. Those conversations were typically saved for evenings hours after work, or simply catching up at family gatherings.

I drove back to the office quickly and still had a few minutes to talk before my next meeting started. I phoned her back from my car as soon as I parked. I decided to simply stay there for our conversation. It was quiet and private, and I knew there in the parking lot we would not be interrupted. When she picked up, her voice was a little shaky.

"What's up?" I asked.

"Well, I had an ultrasound today and everything seems okay. I mean, the baby's healthy."

I could hear the tears beginning to well up over the phone.

"What is it then?" I asked. "What's the matter?"

"The ultrasound showed some concerns."

I listened through the sniffles on the other end of the phone. "And . . .?"

"Well, she is healthy. Everything looked completely normal, except . . ."

"Except what?"

"There's no syndromes and reason for what's happening at all. I've had a completely healthy pregnancy. I've been extremely healthy and everything has been the same as my other pregnancies."

"But...?"

"She's not developing in a normal way. She's perfectly fine, except her limbs aren't developing normally. Our baby doesn't seem to be growing legs."

Then the flood of tears came. My heart sunk. I knew the challenges of missing a leg, but this was a little girl. She was meant to be pretty and wear heels. I began to sink into despair along with her. We sat in silence on the phone, me perplexed and my younger sister in tears.

"She'll be okay," I finally replied. "I don't have a leg. People adapt."

"I know," my sister said as she gained a little more emotional control. "That's why I called you. We just found out and I called you right away."

I just struggled to find what else I could say to comfort her. Sure, I lost a leg, but I had both mine for thirty-three years of life, long enough to experience all the wonderful things youth offered me. I played any sport I wanted to. I walked and ran and grew up with crazy brothers in the great outdoors, hiking, fishing, and going anywhere my legs wanted to take me. I danced and I dated.

"What will her life be like without legs?" my sister asked. "What's it been like for you after losing your left one?"

"She'll be fine," I said, still feeling my heart reeling inside over the news. "They make so many wonderful prosthetics these days. I can assist her through the process. I'll become her favorite uncle." My tone gained a bit more spirit at the end as I attempted to lighten the heavy mood.

I heard all the optimism coming out of my mouth, but my heart was truly troubled. I thought about it all that day and into the night. I shared all kinds of information with my sister about specialists and the prosthetic doctors I had worked with. However, I still lay awake into the darkness of the night contemplating it all. The "why" questions began to rear their heads again.

Why this? Why her? Why our family, again?

It was in the chaos of asking why that clarity actually came: why *not* our family? Who better to love her and see her through this? This little girl would have an amazing mother and father. Her loving siblings that would carry her if they had to, anywhere she'd ever have to go. Then the "what" questions began to replace the why's: what role might I play, and how might I show up for my little niece along her unique journey?

It was as I pondered those thoughts that I felt the energy in the room change. That happened when I knew the veil was opening to shed light onto a situation. I was judging this situation as dark, yet when the energy in the room shifted, I realized it may be the perfect opportunity.

I began to feel the presence of a magnificent soul, a glorious, courageous being. I lay there, simply basking in what I felt when a distinct recognition came: it was Tamara. She was the one coming through on this dark, still night. I felt her as clearly as the other times I had experienced her communicating with me. I closed my eyes in the already dark room simply to feel more. There Tamara was, showing the glory of this new, little soul that was coming into the world. She reminded me that every soul chose and created their journeys here. This was not a tragedy, but a perfect manifestation of free will and choice being honored by the entire universe. That was what unconditional love did; it allowed us to have our experiences without judgment or comparison. It didn't have to look any certain way to be right. Every way was perfect for the soul that had created the journey and chosen to experience it.

"She's a part of me," I heard Tamara whisper to my heart. "I've been with her here and she is amazing. Just wait and see."

Peace filled the entire room, as well as my heart. My little niece is perfect, legs or no legs. Her soul had chosen a unique path, for something her eternal intelligence wanted to experience. Could I not honor that without despair or judgment? Knowing that she was incredibly connected to Tamara was big for me. Are we not all incredibly connected, and might we all be learning by recognizing and honoring each other's journeys?

My niece was born, perfectly, with no legs and only one arm. She is amazing. The beauty and courage of her soul fill an entire room. She is happy, full of laughter, and so powerful. To pretend her life didn't have challenges would be naive, but aren't challenges what make us mighty? And in the end, maybe it was the very things that made us different and unique that actually should be celebrated rather than scorned. For when we truly celebrate our individuality, we discover our own divinity.

CHAPTER 40

I WAS ASKED TO PARTICIPATE at a graduation ceremony at the local high school where Tamara taught. So many years had passed that the administration had changed and much of the faculty had as well. In fact, I was asked to speak completely independent of my relationship with Tamara. I was asked by one of the current student government members, who simply knew me in the community without having ever known Tamara or the details of our story, for that matter. Of course, I graciously agreed to take part and felt honored to be asked. I loved working with young people and when they extended an invitation, I usually made it a priority.

I prepared my remarks in a lose outline format and intended to speak about taking life on with gusto, learning from adversity, and choosing joy whenever possible. I arrived at the high school early. It had been several years since I had been there. The hallways were empty. I could hear my dress shoes clicking on the hard surface of the floor, extenuating my unique gate from the prosthetic. The school had been renovated in many areas, but much of it was exactly the same as I remembered from when Tamara taught there. As I made my way down the long hallway, I noticed the school still had that familiar smell of janitorial cleaning supplies mixed with the thousands of dreams and ambitions of young spirits.

There was a particular part of the high school I wanted to visit. I hoped it was still very much the same, too.

At the time of the accident when Tamara was teaching there, our boys were in the high school daycare. Tamara and others had set up a system where teachers with young children could bring their youngsters to school with them. There was a course set up around early childhood development with two qualified teachers overseeing the class. Students could make it part of their daily class schedule to come in and work with the little ones. It was a fantastic success.

Our boys loved it. Spencer was old enough to tell us at the time how much fun it was as he got a different student assigned to work with him every hour. He got to read, play, talk, and learn all with a new high school aged buddy every fifty minutes. It was a dream for a young, very active and busy boy. Griffin loved it, too. He was cuddled and played with by enthusiastic teens all day while his mom taught in her classroom just moments away. When the little ones cried and fussed, it was also a great education for the high schoolers, giving them a taste of what real parenting might be like while being supervised on how to deal with such things on many different levels.

As part of the course, the high school designated a small, unused atrium as a playground for the daycare kids. It provided a safe, confined place to get fresh air and play outside during the day. When the accident happened and we lost Tamara and Griffin, the students were obviously devastated, especially those who had spent time with Griffin in the daycare.

The faculty and administration decided to dedicate this little playground to the memory of our son and call it "Griffin's Playground." They arranged a dedication and even waited until I was well enough to attend and say a few words. I was touched by their kindness and moved that there would always be a place dedicated to the memory of my little boy. Even as Spencer grew up and entered high school, the playground was still there. In fact, Spencer, as his Eagle Scout Project, updated the playground, replanted more bushes and flowers, and installed a beautiful bench with Griffin's name on it.

That was where I was going before my speech. I hadn't been to Griffin's Playground in years and I wanted to see it.

I found it, much as it had always been, but better. As I peered through the glass windows surrounding the playground I could see that the flowers and bushes Spencer planted had grown in well and the bench was still there. To my surprise, the door was unlocked and I was able to walk into the atrium and sit on the bench. So many years had gone by since the accident. So much had happened. I began counting dates and realized it had been seventeen years.

Then it hit me, and I was ashamed to admit I hadn't realized it until that moment. I had approached this event as simply giving a motivational speech at the local high school until I sat right there, in that sacred little playground, on that blessed bench. Waves of emotion overcame me. Tears welled up uncontrollably in my eyes. This would have been Griffin's graduating class. This would have been his graduation day had the accident not taken him so young, so many years ago.

I began to weep uncontrollably, sitting on that bench all alone. First, I dealt with the shame of not realizing this truth until that very moment. Second, I embraced the gratitude I felt when I realized that the kindness of the universe had placed me here to be a part of it. It was by pure chance that I had been invited on this occasion to address the graduating seniors. Nobody, not even me, had put all the pieces together. And yet here I was, honoring those who would have known my son well had he been here with them. I sat there for some time, crying at the synchronicity of it all.

It was only a few minutes now before I was to meet the folks backstage in the auditorium to prepare for the ceremony. I tried to dry my eyes and gain some resemblance of composure. I also realized people were beginning to fill the hallways outside the atrium showing up for the ceremonies. I made my way to the nearest men's room and quickly washed my face and blew my nose. I rushed as best as I could to the auditorium and found my way backstage through the crowd that was already taking their seats.

The emotions nearly boiling over as I announced to those who needed to know that I was there and ready. I had grabbed tissues from the men's room and stuffed my pockets with them. I stepped back into the shadows again as I nearly lost it one more time, watching all those beautiful seniors entering the auditorium. I wiped my eyes again and took a deep breath as my introduction was made and I stepped out onto the stage.

As I reached the podium and stood under the blinding spotlights, it was all I could do to not lose it. I looked into the faces of those graduates, glancing at those beautiful eighteen-year-old seniors that would have been the teammates, the buddies, and the girlfriends of my son Griffin. What would have he become? What role might he have played among them all? How tall would he have grown? How would he have worn his hair?

And how different would it have been for me if I was a proud parent sitting in the audience rather than a broken man, barely holding it together, having just sat in a playground which was named after his memory where Griffin had actually been days before he left this world. I knew I'd never gotten over the accident, and I supposed I never would. I'd simply gotten used to it, and this was bringing memories and all the emotions to the surface again.

I'm not sure how I got through the speech, but I knew it was much different than the one I had outlined. I sent love to each and every one of those wonderful senior souls. I shared wisdom as if it was an opportunity to speak to Griffin, if he was still here. And somehow, he was; I was not alone on that stage. I felt him there with me as I looked into the eyes of what would have been such a major part of his life. He gifted that to me, to be in that moment that would have been his. And yet it was his, and mine, all in the divine order and timing that only an angel could create.

CHAPTER 41

I T'S STRANGE TO LOOK up at my children. I woke up one day and suddenly, the little boys who rode on my shoulders were all taller than I am. It was even stranger to realize they'd transformed into men.

I watched as they put on their dress shirts and straightened each other's neck ties preparing for Spencer, my oldest son's, wedding nuptials. Spencer and Ashley had fallen madly in love and were being married that early August afternoon in 2015. The day was sunny and warm, yet thunder clouds had been threatening along the mountain tops most of the morning. So far, the day had held the heat of late summer with the promise of refreshing, cool rain. It felt like walking into a live family scrapbook; the sights, the sounds, the smells, and the entire venue were abuzz with family and friends as all the preparations came together. Spencer had selected his two younger brothers among his groomsmen, and it made me proud to watch them as they joked, laughed, and supported each other in matching, formal attire. Aiden was nearly as tall as Spencer by now and Zach too had almost passed me up in stature. I realized they were men. Although there was still plenty of boy-like behavior, my children were actually grown.

Our entire family had arrived for the services. Both sides. Tonya's family had all flown in and had been anxiously engaged in all the preparations. Tonya's mother had spent hours cutting brightly colored prayer ribbons to hang in the large tree Ashley, and Spencer would be married under. My mother and all her sisters had handled the flower arrangements for the wedding, and everything was lovely. Ashley's parents had arranged for a beautiful reception dinner in a vintage mansion that was decorated to the nines where we would gather inside after the outdoor services were complete. Everything was perfect.

We had all come together the evening before for a rehearsal dinner where we got a close peek at the rings. Spencer had actually taken diamonds from his mother, Tamara's ring, and had them included in a spectacular setting for Ashley. Ashley and I discussed Spencer's ring and she had created a beautiful manly design, which had inset a guitar string from her own guitar, which Spencer had picked up and played for her on one of their first dates.

I had offered my original wedding ring to be melted down and used for the band which held the guitar string. As a musician, Spencer loved the ring Ashley designed. I loved that it was the original gold from my ring and that Spencer used some of Tamara's diamonds in Ashley's setting.

Together, they were so thoughtful and creative. It was fun to watch. Ashley had always dreamed of being married under a large tree and her wish was coming true. We put together words on the wedding programs which read:

"Be deeply rooted in love, always reaching higher, toward the light.
Stand strong, yet remain flexible.
Shed that which no longer serves you and transform with each new season into perfect abundance and joy."

Guitar picks had been produced as party favors for all the guests which had a tree motif printed on them with the date along with the simple words, "I pick you." Everything was delightful, and it appeared to be a beautiful day coming together in a grand way. Tonya and I were the first to be seated as we were ushered into the large, shaded area under the tree by Spencer. He hugged me, then hugged Tonya and kissed her on the cheek as he seated us

in the designated chairs in the front row and took his place next to the officiator.

It's difficult to describe the pride of a father as I watched our son, now fully grown, truly in love, and doing what he knew in his heart was right. To witness his confidence, his conviction, and his contentment was only topped by the moment that Ashley was ushered down the aisle by her father. She was stunning, and so happy. She radiated light with every step as we all rose and watched her gracefully take her place next to Spencer. They appeared to me like a king and queen in full majesty, and they read the vows they had written for themselves and made a public commitment to love.

I looked at all my sons standing before me, now as young, full-grown men. Tonya reached around my arm and squeezed it as she saw a small tear of joy well up in my eye. She laid her head softly on my shoulder and squeezed my arm again. She had done such a magnificent job raising our boys. It had not been easy for even one day, and yet here we were. And there they were, in their true splendor.

I counted the three of them and noticed their differences as well as their similarities. They were all my sons, adopted or otherwise. I loved each of them equally and intensely for their own uniqueness. That's when I began to feel that familiar warm rush at the base of my neck and in the small of my back that told me others were there. The large crowd was obviously all seated, but I felt the invisible rush of attendees slip in and take their rightful place in the wedding party.

Great-grandmothers and grandfathers that had long since passed arrived. Friends and family from the other side of everyone involved took their seats. And of course, I felt Griffin take his place next to his brothers. I felt his magnificent soul stand with them in that sacred moment. Then it was Tamara, and she took her place next to Tonya. By then, the small tears welling up in my eyes were a full stream running down both cheeks. What did I do to ever deserve the beautiful angels in my life, on both sides of the veil?

I'm the luckiest man in the world, I thought. *In spite of anything I've seen or been through, I am blessed beyond most.*

As I quickly wiped the tears, an amazing thing happened, something I wouldn't expect anyone to believe had not everyone in attendance experienced the same events. Through the bright, August shafts of light showing through the gathering storm clouds, a beautiful red-tailed hawk began to circle all around the wedding party, the tree, and the seated crowd. She called out two or three times in loud, striking caws for everyone to hear. I knew the souls of our loved ones were there, but this was a manifestation of it to everyone.

Tamara had always loved the film *Ladyhawke*, which came out way back in 1985 while I was living in Scotland and away from her. When I returned home, and throughout our marriage, she'd make me watch it over and over again, which I thought was silly until after I lost her in the accident. Since she left this realm, time and time again throughout my life when I felt her near, red-tailed hawks showed up in the sky. I had even mentioned it to family members on several occasions, and yet here it was, happening right in front of over one hundred people. My tears turned into peaceful joy. I almost let out a chuckle at the feeling of everyone being together and in such harmony. It made me smile simply to know.

Knowing, or to know, is a verb from the Old English word "cnawan." It is to perceive, recognize, be aware or cognizant of. And in that moment, I did; I was aware, I recognized, and I perceived all of it in such a profound way.

The ceremony was perfect. Afterwards we had soft light for all the wedding photographs as the storm clouds continued to gather. By the time we made our way into the magnificent mansion, a tremendous thunderstorm ensued, pouring down buckets of rain which tittered and tattered on the roof in rhythm with the magical music inside as we all ate, danced, and celebrated true love.

CHAPTER 42

LIFE IS A LESSON of true love, or a remembering, perhaps, of the pure love we actually are. I sat on the grass at the cemetery and read the inscription on the headstone: "Bound by golden cords of love." When I had originally done the headstones, I was so bereaved, and even though I was only thirty-three years old, I believed I would never marry again. Now, after so many years and after so much had happened, I felt it was only fitting that Tonya should be represented in the family burial plot.

Being only in our early thirties, Tamara and I had not done any previous planning around death. My mother had stepped in quickly to purchase the burial plots in the chaos of the accident. At the time, they knew they would be burying Tamara and Griffin, and because I was in such rough shape, there was also a high likelihood that they may be burying me as well. Even after the fact when I finally returned home from the hospital, we never really discussed the details of the cemetery arrangements. It had become an event of the past while I was still in critical condition in ICU. My mother most likely told me what she had arranged, and I simply didn't remember all the details.

To my best recollection, she had purchased three burial plots together, with the assumption that there would be one for each of us: Tamara, Griffin, and myself. When I was able to share that Tamara was still communicating with me and wanted to be buried with Griffin in her arms, they were both placed in the same casket together and buried in one plot.

When I was well enough, I designed headstones, but had put Tamara and my names together on a placeholder stone where I intended to be buried someday, leaving only Griffin's name on the plot that actually held both my loved ones. This left two empty burial plots, one for me, and one for Tonya. I even found divine order in that coincidence. Out of respect, love, and honor for Tonya, I wanted to revise the headstones. It felt appropriate that I put both Tamara and Griffin's names on the plot where they were actually buried, revising the second headstone to bare my name, and a third for Tonya.

I called the cemetery business office to see if this was a feasible request. As they pulled up the records, I received some interesting news. Years before, when my mother had so lovingly yet hurriedly purchased the plots in time for the funeral services, she was offered a family plot for only a little extra, which actually contained four burial plots rather than three, along with a tree and a bench to be placed near the headstones. My mother had purchased the family site rather than just the three plots.

This provided an entire new opportunity to not only revise the headstones, but to select a tree to be planted nearby as well as a family bench. It was the perfect solution. I began working with the cemetery to have things revised and put in place. However, proceeding with doing that now, years after the fact, presented some obstacles. First of all, with so many of the adjacent burial plots now full, the grounds crew found it impossible to actually plant the tree simply because there was not enough free space without disrupting nearby burial plots.

We were disappointed, but decided to skip the tree and proceed with the revised headstones and family bench. Additional disappointing news then came that the bench could also not be approved because there were restrictions on the number and proximity of benches in certain areas of the cemetery, including where Tamara and Griffin were buried.

We felt bad, but knew perhaps too much time had passed to make an easy adjustment. The folks at the cemetery were very kind, however. I received a call from them the following Monday as I was driving to work. They explained that there was another option.

"We want you to have what was paid for. You certainly deserve the bench and tree. Perhaps we can provide a solution."

I switched the phone to speaker, set it in the console, and continued to drive while I listened intently as they outlined a potential solution.

"We are opening up a new area of the cemetery where we could easily provide everything you have coming to you."

"What does that mean?" I asked.

"Well, it would mean relocating your loved ones."

"You mean digging them up and reburying them?" I asked hesitantly.

"Yes, but they are in a vault and it should be a very streamlined process if you decide you want to proceed. Otherwise, we can simply leave things as they are and refund you the cost of the tree and bench."

My mind was racing. I didn't want to move them. That seemed morbid to me.

"Why don't you come by this evening and I can show you the new area where we could relocate them if you choose to do so. You can take your time and think it over."

I paused and took a deep breath. "Alright," I said. "I could come by after work, but I'm not sure we want to do anything at this point."

I contemplated the new option throughout the day. I just wasn't sure about any of it. I discussed it with Tonya, and although she left much of the decision to me, she suggested I at least take a look and consider the options.

I drove straight to the cemetery right after work. The gentleman greeted me warmly and offered me a ride in the staff golf cart as we took a look around the cemetery. We first went to the existing burial site. It still evoked great reverence for me to visit. We sat silently in the golf cart for a few minutes, then I walked over to look at the headstones. The cemetery official explained the issues with putting the bench or a tree in that existing area. Even if we used the remaining two burial plots, it was problematic.

I contemplated, but quite honestly was ready to forget the whole thing.

I didn't want to disrupt what had become such a sacred place to me. I didn't respond immediately, and looked out to the west horizon, noticing what was shaping up to be a beautiful sunset.

"Would you like to at least take a look at the new area?" he asked me.

"I suppose," I replied. "That's what I came here for, and you've been very kind. Sure, let's take a look."

We began to drive toward the lower end of the cemetery very near the road, not far from the handicap parking section where I had parked the car when I arrived. There was a clearing of lawn with thick scrub oak growing along the edge of it. I was almost drawn to the spot as if I knew that's where we were going. Sure enough, we parked the golf cart in the large clearing and the gentleman began to explain the options to me. I was hardly listening.

It's so close to the road and the parking, I thought.

"This is the new area. We could very efficiently relocate them here free of charge to you and most certainly do the family bench and tree in this area if you choose to do so."

I stepped out of the golf cart and walked on the soft grass, making my way toward the thick trees. The shade was cool in the setting sun. *I don't want to move them*, I thought, then it hit me, almost like a jolt: I heard Tamara's voice whispering truth to my heart.

"You never got the chance to bury me and Griffin, my love. You missed all of it with very little closure at all. It was done while you lay fighting for your life in the hospital."

I felt the tears begin to well up in my eyes, which almost always happened when communication came in such a way.

"You never got to say your peace," Tamara continued. "You never got to touch the casket or toss a flower. And you didn't receive the closure other family members did. This is my gift to you, if you choose to receive it. You can dedicate the grave in your way, in your words, with your spirit and your power, and say good-bye in the traditional ways of this realm."

I just stood there in the setting sun, contemplating the possibility. The gentleman from the cemetery gave me my space as if he could sense I was experiencing something profound. I liked the way this new location felt, but was it too close to the parking area? Then, suddenly that too came into perspective; the current burial site was half way down a fairly steep hill. Aging family members had a difficult time getting to the graves and even I found it challenging to visit the burial site as often as I used to.

Moving them to the new location would make it much easier for me and others to visit. No hill to hike, convenient parking nearby, and with plenty of shade from the trees along the edge of the area. My body was aging too, and the results of my injuries were manifesting more and more. As time passed for me, it would not be any easier to get to the existing grave site. This actually could be the perfect location for me to still easily come visit, and often. I took my mobile phone out and dialed Spencer's number.

"Hi, Son, it's Dad."

"Hey Dad, what's up?"

"Well, I'm up at the cemetery."

I explained the entire circumstances; the bench, the tree, and the possibility of moving the burial site. Spencer listened intently.

"I don't want to tear open any wounds for you, Son," I said honestly. "I know it may seem strange to move the grave site, but I've had something come to me here, and I'm considering it. If we do this, I would have the opportunity to take part in what I was never able to do. I know that may sound selfish, but I could dedicate the graves and perhaps create some closure."

I listened carefully as Spencer responded. I could sense some tender emotions in his voice from the other end of the phone.

"Dad, it's a beautiful idea," Spencer said. "I was so little and so young. I didn't understand what was going on that day so many years ago. I was avoiding it all, pretending that maybe it didn't really happen. To take part in a meaningful way now, as a grown man, and to do it together, privately, and yet very personally, would give me closure I never got as a little boy."

I knew it was meant to be in my son's response. The sky was now blazed a brilliant orange in the autumn sunset. How quickly my mind had been changed by feeling Tamara's message and by hearing what Spencer had to say. I reached out and touched the colorful fall leaves on the trees lining the proposed burial site. I quickly called Tonya and told her how I felt. She agreed it was the best decision. I made my way back to the golf cart where the cemetery official had waited so patiently and began making the arrangements.

CHAPTER 43

THE MORNING WAS COOL and crisp. I could easily see my breath as I finished dressing on the back deck overlooking the canyon view. I put on my favorite formal, knee length coat, one I had kept all these years since I purchased it in Scotland clear back in 1986 while living there. I ran my hands over the thick charcoal wool, did up the large pewter buttons, and prepared to go to the cemetery early. We decided to make it a very private event, and I wanted to be there for the entire process. The morning was crisp but sunny. It was the Saturday after Thanksgiving. I met the grounds crew at the cemetery, who had already prepared the new burial plot. They even put up a small canopy and set out chairs even though there would only be a few of us.

I wanted to be there as they exposed the vault and moved it to the new location. Spencer and Ashley joined me as well. Everything went beautifully. The vault was in perfect condition, even after almost twenty years. It was easily moved to the new site and placed on the casket rack.

It was difficult to explain the emotions of what I chose to witness. I was flooded with deep feelings of gratitude and love as the vault was raised up. They felt so close. I kept imagining the vault would open and they'd joyfully climb out and join us as if none of this ever happened. I walked over and put my hand on the vault.

It was cool and smooth to the touch, but seemed so alive as I ran my hand over concrete curves. I wanted to send all my love, my blessings, and my energy to them somehow. I wanted them to feel my gratitude. I knew it was simply the container of their remains, but it felt to me as if they were there.

My experiences over the years had proven that they were alive and well, time after time. However, knowing that their remains were right there before me opened up a very sacred and emotional space. I remembered Tamara's stunning blues eyes and how it felt to hold her hand. I thought of her feet, and how lightly and gracefully she walked. I remembered Griffin's little baby slobber kisses he would give me, cutting his hair for the first time, and his mischievous smile which mimicked his mother's, that both he and Tamara flashed often and with ease.

They were both there in spirit as real as if they had joyfully come out of the vault. Many others from the heavenly realms were there with them. It was like a grand reunion of life through the veil. They sent love to all of us, letting us know they were here, watching over us, always.

My thoughts then turned to Tonya and how supportive and patient she had been with me over all these years. I'd now been married to Tonya far longer than I was ever married to Tamara. She had walked with me through so much healing and finding my way. I remembered it was my desire to add her name on the headstone next to mine which actually instituted this whole ordeal of relocating the burial site in the first place.

Silent tears streamed down my face now. I could hardly maintain my composure. I had no idea I would be so emotional after all this time, but my heart was as open as the grave plot, raw and ready to receive, as the flood of memories and blessings came pouring in.

Spencer remained stoic and strong, putting his arm around me as I wept. His wife, Ashley, also came to my side to comfort me. We placed white roses and quartz crystals on the vault. I had also cut fresh sage, mint, and lavender from our back hill to add to the white roses. After all the flowers and herbs were placed, I kissed my hand and put it again firmly on the vault. Spencer sent his blessings and love by adding personal items he brought to the top of the vault.

We stood there, arm-in-arm as they lowered it into the ground. Tears ran down both our cheeks now. He was a grown man, experiencing the same love for his wife that I had lost when losing Tamara. Somehow, I felt that now he knew more and understood at much deeper levels what I had been through over the years. I felt his hand squeeze my shoulder. The little boy who lost so much was now full grown and being the stronger one for his dad. We knelt down and in our own way dedicated the graves as the final resting place for Tamara and Griffin. I could barely speak through the emotion as I attempted to convey what I wanted to say. Spencer put a strong hand in the center of my back as I struggled through the tears to express what words could never say.

When we were finished, I knelt a little longer than the others. Spencer finally assisted me to my feet. We stood and looked for a long time at the vault, flowers, and all the personal items resting in the earth. The grounds crew was patient, as this wasn't a typical burial ceremony. They were simply there to move the vault and do their job, but they were peaceful as we paid our respects. There were two shovels standing up in the pile of soil left from the open cemetery plot. I looked at Spencer and, without saying a word, we both knew what to do.

We walked over to the shovels and began gently throwing dirt onto the vault. It seemed fitting that we do the honor of burying them. It was not work, but a privilege. We lovingly offered shovels full of soil as if we were making sacred offerings of love, gratitude, and memories onto their grave until the entire top of the vault was covered.

Closure? Perhaps. Although it was deeply emotional, it was healing in many ways. Spencer and I took part in something we missed so many years ago. Spencer, because he was so young and avoiding the pain in every way he could. Me, because I was in ICU fighting for my life, which I wasn't even sure I wanted at the time, except to raise the son who was now a man standing next to me. I would have never believed we could have gotten to this place.

It was interesting to me that we lost Tamara and Griffin the day after Easter, a holiday of resurrection and rebirth, and now, nearly twenty years later, we were re-burying them just a day after Thanksgiving, a holiday of gratitude. Fitting, given how thankful I was. It may seem strange to say thankful, but truly I was. It was incredible to have loved like I have loved, to be loved as I am, and to have learned so much through the process.

I was once asked what I learned from all the loss, all the experiences, all the heartaches, and all the triumphs. My spirit seemed to answer before my brain could. Before I even knew my mouth was open, I heard myself say, "Compassion!" I got compassion, the blessed opportunity to feel, and to perhaps in some small way, know what others may be feeling, too.

Do I still have bad days and challenges? Yes, of course; to say my life is void of challenges would be untrue. However, I know from that deepest sacred place within me that all is well and always will be.

To trust is peace, to love is perfect, and to know is divine.

EPILOGUE

DREAMS, VISIONS, AND MIRACLES continue for me today: vivid, poignant, and always with a message. Some say recognizing them like I do is a gift I may have brought back from my near-death experience so many years ago. Others say that those having crossed over and returned experience open channels to receive such things more easily, as if the door to the other realms never completely closed. For me, it's far more about life than it will ever be about death. The causes or reasons don't matter to me; I am simply grateful to have the insights.

I've come a long way since the loss of my life at mile marker 80. What began there is still unfolding in magnificent ways. I've learned the universe does nothing to me, but for me. It lovingly supports me, without judgment, as I make my choices, create my life experience, and grow.

I've learned that true joy comes through the simple things in life—the way my wife's toes touch my leg under the covers in the morning, feeling the laughter of my sons, buying a twelve-dollar hummingbird feeder and watching the birds gather to it. Looking for happiness in big things usually leaves me empty, while embracing life's beautiful, little miracles fills my heart with joy and gratitude. And by the way, there are no little miracles. A winter morning sunrise or a summer evening rainstorm are equal to water turned to wine from my perspective.

When hope and faith have waned and only despair remains, we are perhaps in our most beautiful state. It is in this space that complete trust arises, and a willingness to accept what is, and be honest about it.

I've learned that being perfect has nothing to do with how many or how few mistakes I make. In fact, there actually are no mistakes, only the process. It's not about the finished puzzle, but searching the shape of the individual edges and enjoying the little discoveries. Therein lies the perfection.

There is little to do and much more to simply be. Look to the light and blossom. "Consider the lilies of the field, how they grow; they do not toil, neither do they spin." (Matthew 6:28–29). We are the lilies. We are the beautiful manifestations of the divine, simply growing and pointing upward toward home. I returned to that home and stood in the presence of deity, and yet peace only came when I began to remember the divinity within myself.

I used to believe God was testing me in some way and wanted me to prove my faith somehow. I have come to a deeper truth; God isn't testing me at all. God knows me perfectly. It was *me* who didn't know myself. We come from perfect love, and we will return to it someday, but for now, we love imperfectly, beautifully flawed in this lower dimension. Yet our skinned knees and scraped palms are not signs of shame, but rather badges of courage for having come to play the game. We are beautiful in our brokenness and perfect in the chaos regardless of the judgments we may put on it. Each moment is sacred. Each moment is a gift. Life is not a test. Life is a gift.

Every little thing is of the light; there is divine order in every single experience and every soul who crosses my path. Everything in my existence has a gift for me, otherwise it would not be so. Being open to that divine gift in each and every moment is what brings life profound meaning.

Recognize it.
Feel it.
Embrace it.
Know it.

A very special thanks to Tracy Coen.

Her support is the epitome of trust, compassion, and "knowing."

ABOUT THE AUTHOR

J EFFERY C. OLSEN IS a bestselling author and moving public speaker, inspiring audiences internationally with his intriguing stories of perseverance and inner strength.

In 1997, Olsen experienced a horrific automobile accident that took the lives of both his wife and youngest son. He suffered multiple life-threatening injuries himself, including the amputation of his left leg above the knee. As a result of the accident, Jeffery had profound out of body, shared-death and near-death experiences, which give him spiritual insights not common in today's world.

In addition to his live stage appearances around the world, Olsen has appeared on numerous national and international television and radio programs sharing his inspirational insights.

Professionally, Olsen is a gifted Creative Director with accolades from the New York One Show, the Clio Awards, Communication Arts and The American Advertising Federation just to name a few. He has appeared in Forbes Magazine, has been on the Inc. 500 list and is an Earnst & Young Entrepreneur of the Year Finalist, demonstrating a winning combination of talent and tenacity.

Olsen enjoys spending time outdoors simply observing the natural beauty of this world. His greatest joy however is found in being a husband, father and friend.

www.EnvoyPublishing.com

CPSIA information can be obtained
at www.ICGtesting.com
Printed in the USA
LVHW111008250619
622284LV00001B/70/P